The Journey to PURPOSE: Navigating *your* Spiritual Path

Jerry M. Carter, Jr. Ph. D.

The Journey to Purpose: Navigating Your Spiritual Path
By Jerry M. Carter, Jr. Ph. D.

© 2019 Jerry M. Carter, Jr. Ph. D.

For information, address:

The Church Online, LLC
1000 Ardmore Blvd.
Pittsburgh, PA 15221

International Standard Book Number: 978-1-940786-80-3

Library of Congress Catalogue Number: Available Upon Request

All scripture quotations are taken from the Holy Bible, New International Version®, NIV®. Copyright © 1973, 1978, 1984, 2011 by Biblica, Inc.™ unless otherwise noted. Used by permission of Zondervan. All rights reserved worldwide. www.zondervan.com The "NIV" and "New International Version" are trademarks registered in the United States Patent and Trademark Office by Biblica, Inc.™

Printed in the United States of America

Trademarks

All terms mentioned in this book that are known to be or are suspected of being trademarks or service marks have been appropriately capitalized. Use of a term in this book should not be regarded as affecting the validity of any trademark or service mark.

Published by The Church Online, LLC

ACKNOWLEDGEMENTS

Special thanks to Rev. Monica A. Ashley, Executive Director
Jerry M. Carter, Jr. Ministries, LLC for her creativity and vision,
and organization and management of the book project. To
Rev. Dr. David A. Hollowell for his editorial skills and expertise
in Christian Education and curriculum development.

DEDICATION

I would like to dedicate this book to my children
Jerry M. III, Zachary Daniel and Camille, the Calvary Church
family, my colleagues and co-laborers in ministry who serve
as constant sources of inspiration and encouragement.

To the churches, campus ministries, small groups and
individual readers, may this work be a lamp unto your feet
and a light illuminating pathways in your journey to purpose.

To my parents, who assisted me in my journey to purpose,
I dedicate this book in loving memory of you. Gone but not
forgotten. Until we meet again.

Jerry M. Carter, Sr. [December 2018]

Gloria J. Carter [April 2019]

TABLE OF CONTENTS

CHAPTER 1

IT'S NOT TOO LATE TO START THE JOURNEY

Have you ever wondered about your purpose in life? Have you ever questioned why you are here on Earth? Have you had doubts, and even fears, about where your life is heading?

Every one of us has periodic bouts of frustration and angst about our role and position in the universe. At one end of the spectrum, we can become fatalistic, relinquish any control over our lives, and allow people and circumstances to shape our future. On the other end, we can attempt to take total control of our fate by forcing our decisions and actions on other people and the world around us. Then there's the middle ground, where we fluctuate between being controlled and taking control. Over the course of time, we come to realize that defining our purpose in life is a lifelong journey over this middle ground.

Journey to Purpose uses the Bible, specifically the Book of Exodus, to demonstrate how you, too, can journey toward and live your true purpose in life. The Book of Exodus is the story of the journey of the Israelites from a life of slavery and exile to one of freedom and purpose. The word "exodus" means the departure of a multitude of people, particularly emigrants, those who have left their home country. The Israelites must endure and persevere through fear, doubt, uncertainty, and hardships that can only be overcome by God's intervention to fulfill God's ultimate purpose and promise. By examining the life, challenges, mistakes, and victories of Moses, the man God chose to lead the Israelites out of Egypt, this study guide can help you navigate your own journey to purpose. Through the experiences of Moses and the Israelites, we can acquire a deeper understanding of ourselves, our choices, and the circumstances that shape our journey.

Each chapter includes:

- a guided tour of the Biblical text dealing with an aspect of our journey.
- key points summarizing the main takeaways from the text.
- questions to reflect on the key scripture and apply it in today's context.
- questions to reflect on your journey and help you discover your unique path to purpose.
- a prayer to guide you toward God during each phase of your journey.

Let's begin exploring your purpose by studying the journey that Moses takes—starting with the circumstances of his birth. Read Exodus Chapters 1 and 2.

GOD'S PURPOSE: GOD HAD BIG PLANS FOR MOSES.

In Chapter 1 of Exodus, the Israelites were growing too strong and numerous compared to the original people of the land (Exodus 1:1-22). The Israelites are the descendants of Abraham (the father of many nations) through his son Isaac and his son Jacob. God changes Jacob's name to Israel (Genesis 32:28), and his descendants become the Israelites. They are also known as Hebrews, Jews, and God's chosen people.

Now, the best way to weaken a people is to remove the men. So, Pharaoh, the king of Egypt, issues an edict to kill all the newborn males of the Israelite families to get rid of the boys who would later become men.

"Look," he said to his people, "the Israelites have become far too numerous for us. Come, we must deal shrewdly with them or they will become even more numerous and, if war breaks out, will join our enemies, fight against us and leave the country." (Exodus 1:9-10)

11

Then Pharaoh gave this order to all his people: "Every Hebrew boy that is born you must throw into the Nile, but let every girl live." (Exodus 1:22)

In Chapter 2 of Exodus, Moses' mother, Jochebed, decides that she will not listen to the king of the country because there was another King above that king who orders her life. She hides baby Moses for three months. When he starts making too much noise, she has to come up with another plan.

The plan was to make a basket with tar around it and set it afloat on the crocodile-infested Nile River with Moses' sister watching over him (Clearly, God had big plans for Moses!). One day, Pharaoh's daughter was bathing in the river. She sees the basket and calls her servants to get it. When Moses is taken up by Pharaoh's daughter, Moses' sister goes over to her and asks, "Would you like for me to get one of the Hebrew women to come and nurse the young child?" Pharaoh's daughter says yes, so of course Moses' sister got Moses' mother to become Moses' nurse—and get paid for it, too!

Pharaoh's daughter said to her, "Take this baby and nurse him for me, and I will pay you." So the woman took the baby and nursed him. When the child grew older, she took him to Pharaoh's daughter and he became her son. She named him Moses, saying, "I drew him out of the water." (Exodus 2:9–10)

God had big plans for Moses. Moses, nursed by his mother, ends up growing up in Pharaoh's household. He is afforded all the privileges and luxuries of an Egyptian lifestyle. He is exposed to Egyptian customs, learns the Egyptian language, goes to an Egyptian private school, and graduates from the Egyptian university. He climbs his way up the corporate ladder and is given a job in management by Pharaoh.

MISTAKES WILL BE MADE, BUT THE JOURNEY CONTINUES.

Even though Moses is blessed with all the luxuries and privileges of a king and the Egyptians, he never forgets his identity. He understands at the heart that he is a Hebrew and that the majority of his people are not *living* in Pharaoh's household—they are oppressed. With true empathy, he experiences the pain and frustration of being subjugated and oppressed. One day when he sees one of his Hebrew brothers suffering at the hand of an Egyptian, he kills the Egyptian.

One day, after Moses had grown up, he went out to where his own people were and watched them at their hard labor. He saw an Egyptian beating a Hebrew, one of his own people. Looking this way and that and seeing no one, he killed the Egyptian and hid him in the sand. (Exodus 2:11–12)

13

Everybody looking from the outside in would call this a random act of senseless violence from another "Hebrew thug." But it's the context of injustice and subjugation that has led to this act. We can't condone this murder on Moses' part, but if we look at the context of the Hebrews' situation, we can see the reasons why it happened. We also can't deal with the violence of Moses without dealing with the injustice of the Egyptian system that gave birth to the Moseses of the world, who only know how to express their frustration through dysfunctional acts.

Moses murders this Egyptian, buries him in the sand, and thinks it's over. However, when he breaks up another fight—this time between two Hebrews—Moses discovers that what he thought was buried in the sand wasn't really gone.

The next day he went out and saw two Hebrews fighting. He asked the one in the wrong, "Why are you hitting your fellow Hebrew?"

The man said, "Who made you ruler and judge over us? Are you thinking of killing me as you killed the Egyptian?" Then Moses was afraid and thought, "What I did must have become known." (Exodus 2:13–14)

Not only do these two Hebrews know what happened, but Pharaoh finds out and now Pharaoh is after Moses' life (see Exodus 2:15–25).

Moses flees to a place called Midian. End of story. It's done—right? Another brother filled with potential has become a statistic. Another Sonia Sotomayor is benched before she can become a justice of the Supreme Court. Another potential liberator is now sitting on the sidelines. God had special things planned for Moses, but now one act of violence, a senseless act of passion, has sidelined him. Perhaps, like many of us would, Moses is feeling hopeless and ready to concede to his present fate. What now?

Is Moses' journey to purpose over? Has he messed up so badly that he can never fulfill his intended purpose? Should he listen to his friends, family, or the enemy and chuck his dreams into a hearse, drive to the cemetery, deposit them six feet under, and listen to somebody say, "Ashes to ashes and dust to dust"?

Maybe, like Moses, you've made mistakes, too. Maybe you feel as if you've wasted too much time or are too old to accomplish God's plan. But just when you think your story is over, maybe it's not too late after all. Maybe it's not done when you think it's done. Don't close the book, because the story continues.

THE JOURNEY SOMETIMES LEADS TO SHEPHERDING IN THE WASTELAND.

Moses murdered an Egyptian man and flees to Midian, but God is still guiding his journey to purpose. While Moses is sitting beside a well, the scenes of his life are being directed by God when the right people appear.

> *Now the priest of Midian had seven daughters who came as usual to draw water and fill the water troughs for their father's flocks. But some other shepherds came and chased them away. So Moses jumped up and rescued the girls from the shepherds. Then he drew water for their flocks. (Exodus 2:16–17)*

The daughters of the priest of Midian go back and tell their father, Jethro (also called Rueul), and he invites Moses to become a part of the household. Moses marries Zipporah, one of Jethro's daughters. They have children, and he ends up with a job as a shepherd.

Something is wrong with this picture. Exodus Chapter 2 describes the birth of a budding, blossoming hero of the nation who's going to liberate people. Moses stands up to injustice twice.

First, he stops a beating (Exodus 2:11–12). Then, he rescues Jethro's daughters (Exodus 2:16–17). But then he becomes a shepherd in the desert. This is where his mistakes have landed him. He is literally the leader of sheep.

Now, there is absolutely nothing wrong with being a shepherd, but this wasn't God's big plan. The Lord God had not protected Moses when he was three months old, guarded him against the dangerous crocodile-infested waters of the Nile, raised him in Pharaoh's household, and afforded him the privilege of an Egyptian lifestyle for him to be a shepherd.

God had intended more for Moses, but Midian and shepherding is where his life choices had landed him. And, most of the time, Moses was alright with being a shepherd. But, from time to time, there might have been nights during which he would gaze into the sky and wistfully long for *what could have been*. It's painful and disconcerting to have to deal with what could have been.

Have you ever been there? Have you had days when you gaze into the Midian sky wondering what could have been? Maybe you believe you ought to be further along than you are right now—that you ought to be doing something different right now, with somebody else right now, working somewhere else right now, earning a certain income right now. Maybe you believe your life is purpose-*less* right now.

If we're honest, all of us, at some point, have been where Moses was. Moses' life experience shows us that it takes a long time to *build* our lives, but only seconds to *mess* them up! One decision can have you living in the basement when you were created to live life in the penthouse. One decision can have you riding in coach when you were made to be in first class. All it takes is one decision.

Moses is leading sheep in Mount Horeb. "Horeb" in Hebrew means wasteland. Moses' choices have led him to the wasteland. Time is wasted. Money is wasted. Energy is wasted. Imagination and potential are wasted. This is his present circumstance, but God's grace does not leave him there.

PRESENT CIRCUMSTANCE CAN BE CHANGED BY NEW PURPOSE.

Moses' present circumstance is changed because God shows up in the form of a burning bush (Exodus 3:1-10), invades the narrative of Moses' life, and infuses it with a new purpose. This purpose is revealed to Moses immediately. For some of us, it happens that way—an immediate and impactful message from God. For others, the delivery is a gradual discovery and revelation.

Moses' life is changed!

Think about that: just when you have settled for your own history, God will interrupt with a new purpose. The presence of God can invade even *your* wasteland. Even if you are living in circumstances that you know are beneath you, God knows how to find you where you are. One of the joyful realities of living is that God knows how to locate you even in remote places and isolated seasons.

Are you living in Horeb?

Horeb is where you're not supposed to be. Horeb is where you can become secure with living a life that is not the life you are meant to live. You know it. God knows it.

God knows how to find you in Horeb to give you a renewed sense of purpose.

DELAYED PURPOSE DOES NOT MEAN DESTROYED PURPOSE.

In Horeb, the Lord tells Moses, "I know where you've been and I know what you've done, but I'm coming to you anyway." God is saying that delayed purpose does not mean destroyed purpose. God basically tells Moses: "I know you have become satisfied with being a shepherd of sheep, but I want you to become a liberator of people."

19

God tells us: "This is where I wanted you the whole time. Your mistakes have delayed where I want you to be, but they have not destroyed what I want you to be doing. I know you've spent some wasted days, and I know you've gone in some wrong directions, but I want you to know that I still have purpose for you. I know you don't think you're worth anything anymore. I know you've spent most of your life regretting what you've done. But I still have purpose for you."

The fact that God awakened you this morning means that God still has purpose for you. God is not wasting time. God still has something for you to do.

God does not forget what *can be,* even when you have settled for what *is.* "Can be" is in God's vocabulary. "Can be" is a part of God's being. God never forgets what "can be"—no matter where you've gone, no matter what you've done, no matter how many days you've wasted. God is always focused on what "can be," ultimately, what you are becoming.

DETOURS DON'T CHANGE YOUR DESTINATION.

Moses' circumstances teach us the journey towards purpose includes detours, but the detours do not change our destination. It was not a part of the original plan for Moses to spend twenty years in Midian. Midian was a detour. The fact that Moses had to take this detour did not change his ultimate destination. His ultimate destination was to become a liberator of the people of Israel, but he had to take the detour.

There are times when we have to take detours, and sometimes it may take longer. Some detours we cause ourselves, but thank God that they never change the destination. You might give up on the destination, but the detours have not changed God's plan for your life.

DETOURS AND DELAYS CAN BE DAYS OF DEVELOPMENT.

Moses' circumstances also teach us that detours and delays can be days of development. While Moses was in Midian, what was he doing? He was tending sheep. And what would he be doing when he discovered his purpose? He would be leading an oppressed people out of the captivity of Pharaoh's rule to freedom and a new land. And the Israelites were not just any people, but a Nation chosen by God. Don't think that God didn't already have that in mind. God did not cause this delay, but God allowed it because the days Moses spent tending sheep would get him ready to lead the people.

Even though Moses was spending time that he thought might be wasted time, God does not believe in wasted time. You may not know why God allowed you to go through certain seasons, but looking back, you can thank God that you went through what you went through because you learned valuable lessons during the delay. There are some things you learned in that detour that you could not learn in church. There are some things you learned in that season that you could not learn on the job. There are some things that you learned in Midian that you could not learn in Pharaoh's palace.

God does not waste those experiences. God uses what you've been through to get you where he really wants you to be. For God, it's never too late. For you, it's never too late. You're still on the path to purpose.

GOD IS THE AUTHOR AND FINISHER OF YOUR LIFE'S STORY.

When Moses is in Midian, God is preparing to write the next chapter in Moses' story. We might think it's too late for sheep-tending Moses. Moses probably thought it was too late for sheep-tending Moses.

But the Lord showed up and continued his story. And God will show up and continue your story. You might think your story is over, but don't let anybody else write the next (or even the final) chapter to your story. And don't try to write it yourself. God is the only one who should have the right to write the last chapter in your story.

Most everyone thought that the story of Jesus was over on Friday. Pilate, the Roman governor who ordered Jesus' death, thought he had written the last chapter to Jesus' story. Caiaphas, the high priest who organized the plot to kill Jesus, thought he had written the last chapter to the story. The soldiers who rolled the stone over the tomb thought they had written the last chapter. The guard sitting on top of the stone positioned at the grave thought that he was writing the last chapter. That story was buried on Friday night, and everyone believed Jesus' story had ended.

But there was a shift on Resurrection Sunday morning. Our Lord took out His pen and started writing the next chapter. It was titled, "Jesus Lives!"

Don't let past choices, mistakes, or circumstances write the next chapter in your story; let God write it.

Are you ready for the next chapter?

KEY POINTS

- God has a purpose for us; our biggest challenges are discovering and committing to that purpose.

- We are prone to make mistakes when we confuse our purpose with God's purpose.

- Our decisions can cause our purpose to be delayed, or even take a detour, but they do not destroy our purpose.

- God can use delays and detours to develop His purpose for us and get us back on track.

REFLECT ON THE SCRIPTURE

When Pharaoh heard of this, he tried to kill Moses, but Moses fled from Pharaoh and went to live in Midian, where he sat down by a well. (Exodus 2:15)

1. In orchestrating the exodus, was God shaping a purpose for the enslaved Israelites or for Moses?

2. What evidence do you see that God had a purpose for Moses' life?

3. Was Moses' act of violence in murdering the Egyptian in keeping with God's purpose?

4. Did fleeing to Midian for 40 years weaken or strengthen Moses' purpose?

REFLECT ON YOUR JOURNEY

1. Do you feel as if you are living up to the potential of your purpose in life? Why or why not?

2. When in your life have you been satisfied with being a "shepherd of sheep" instead of a liberator of yourself or others?

3. Review Exodus 2:11–15. Are you currently (or have you ever been) in a wasteland, like Horeb? If so, what choices or circumstances took you there?

4. What events have *delayed* or *detoured* your purpose in life? What did you learn or develop during those delays and detours?

5. Did the delays and detours of life change your destination or purpose? Why or why not?

6. Right here, right now: Do you really want to know God's purpose or plan for you? Why or why not?

PRAYER FOR THE JOURNEY

Gracious God, we thank You for placing us here on this Earth and for giving us a purpose in Your Kingdom. We realize that we make mistakes and often run away from what You have asked us to do. Please forgive our stubbornness and the sin of willfulness that seeks our way and not Yours. As we travel on this lifelong journey, we ask that You open our hearts and minds to understanding Your purpose for us. Help us to seek and fulfill Your plan for our lives and be a blessing to others. We pray this in Jesus' name, the One who saves. Amen.

CHAPTER 2

A Name for Right Now

It's possible to settle for something with which you are not satisfied. Sometimes we settle for what we're not satisfied with because we lower our standards or feel like we can't do any better. Sometimes we settle for what we're not satisfied with because "staying put" provides security. Many of us have settled for what we're not satisfied with, and we're so good at it that we even trick ourselves into thinking we *might* be satisfied with it. Don't mistake settling with satisfaction.

There are seasons in life during which we adjust to situations that we really don't want or that we know are not good for us.

In Chapter 2 of the Book of Exodus, it appears as though Moses has settled for leading sheep in a place called Midian (see Exodus 2:11-21). After growing up in Pharaoh's palace and committing a crime in Egypt, he becomes a husband, a father, and a shepherd in Midian.

But Moses was meant for more than this. He settled for shepherding in Midian even though he probably was not satisfied with it.

27

During that long period, the king of Egypt died. The Israelites groaned in their slavery and cried out, and their cry for help because of their slavery went up to God. God heard their groaning and he remembered his covenant with Abraham, with Isaac and with Jacob. So God looked on the Israelites and was concerned about them. (Exodus 3:23-25)

God had another purpose for Moses. Read Exodus Chapter 3.

SOMETIMES, GOD USES A BURNING BUSH TO GET OUR ATTENTION.

One day, as Moses is simply living out his life, he sees something that is physically impossible: a flame burning in a bush that did not burn up. The bush "hosting" the flame wasn't consumed.

Now Moses was tending the flock of Jethro his father-in-law, the priest of Midian, and he led the flock to the far side of the wilderness and came to Horeb, the mountain of God. There the angel of the Lord appeared to him in flames of fire from within a bush. Moses saw that though the bush was on fire it did not burn up. So Moses thought, "I will go over and see this strange sight—why the bush does not burn up." (Exodus 3:1-3)

Now, God can't say anything to Moses until He first gets his attention. No matter what God has to say, unless Moses is focused on God, he can't hear God. Moses first has to give God his undivided attention.

When the Lord saw that he had gone over to look, God called to him from within the bush, "Moses! Moses!" (Exodus 3:4)

When God wants to move us closer toward our purpose, God will seize our attention. When we get stuck on what *is*, instead of leaning toward what *can be*, God will get our attention by any means necessary. God knew a burning bush would get Moses' attention. Only then did God start speaking.

The Lord said, "I have indeed seen the misery of my people in Egypt. I have heard them crying out because of their slave drivers, and I am concerned about their suffering. So I have come down to rescue them from the hand of the Egyptians and to bring them up out of that land into a good and spacious land, a land flowing with milk and honey—the home of the Canaanites, Hittites, Amorites, Perizzites, Hivites and Jebusites. And now the cry of the Israelites has reached me, and I have seen the way the Egyptians are oppressing them. So now, go. I am sending you to Pharaoh to bring my people the Israelites out of Egypt." (Exodus 3:7–10)

The cry of the people has seized heaven's attention. It's difficult for God to see and hear the cry of His children. It's impossible for God not to be concerned. But God goes one step further. He says: "I've seen, I've heard, I'm concerned, and I'm coming down to free them and deliver them to the Promised Land."

Moses is all for God intervening in human history and dismantling injustice. Moses is concerned for his people, and he wants to see them free as well. So, when the Lord says He is going to step into the situation, Moses is overjoyed.

However, there is a shift when God informs Moses that Moses himself would be the one to go and lead the people out of Egypt. Moses did not know that God was going to use him as the instrument of liberation. He was alright with the liberation thing as long as he didn't have to be a part of it. In fact, it seems as if Moses wanted to champion the cause of the oppressed as long as he could do it from a distance.

There are certain causes that we are all for—until they require our personal participation. We can believe in education and growing our spiritual life in theory, but it's different when we're actually challenged to attend church—or read and reflect on this Bible study resource, for example. "Causes" in theory are one thing; "causes" in practice are something else.

When Moses heard that God wanted to send him to deal with Pharaoh, he probably started stuttering. The first thing out of his mouth is "Who am I?" This new challenge for Moses caused him to think about who he was—a liar, a murderer, a criminal (see Exodus 2:11-15). In the words of Robert McAfee Brown, "Moses ducks and weaves in every possible way to avoid the body blow of the assignment."

God responds in a way that again captures Moses' attention.

And God said, "I will be with you. And this will be the sign to you that it is I who have sent you: When you have brought the people out of Egypt, you will worship God on this mountain." (Exodus 3:12)

Suddenly, Moses turns a different direction; now he wants to know who God is. Moses, being a good leader, anticipates the questions of his people.

Moses said to God, "Suppose I go to the Israelites and say to them, 'The God of your fathers has sent me to you,' and they ask me, 'What is his name?' Then what shall I tell them?" (Exodus 3:13).

Moses is considering the possibility of stepping into and fulfilling his God-given purpose. He is considering doing what God is commanding. But, before he returns to the land from which he fled and where not everyone might know him, he wants to be armed with the right information. Moses is not just asking this question for the sake of the people; he wants to know God's name as well.

In Moses' situation, wouldn't you want to know who God is, too? On the journey to purpose, it helps to know (as much as we can) who God is. God is our primary resource, the source of our strength. It's critical to be in touch with God as we journey. Moses wanted to be sure that he wasn't journeying alone. No sports team enters a game and leaves the number one player or primary resource on the sidelines. Moses didn't do that; we shouldn't either. The journey is too difficult. There are too many temptations, distractions, and pitfalls to attempt it alone. Therefore, we need to have some idea of who God is.

SOME OF US NEED TO BE REINTRODUCED TO GOD.

When the Lord found Moses, He had to reintroduce Himself to him. It's very likely that time and suffering had disrupted both Moses' and the Israelites' closeness to God. Where they were in life could have caused them to drift away from their knowledge of God.

It's like going to your high school reunion. One of the biggest challenges is remembering everybody's name. Often, we don't remember names because it's been over twenty or thirty years since we've seen most (if not all) of our classmates.

The Israelites hadn't been around God for much longer than that—430 years, according to Exodus 12:40—so it's very possible that they might not remember His name. Each generation of Israelites, born in Egypt and living in captivity for so long, might have lost a sense of the divine and needed to be reminded who God was.

Succeeding generations can tend to drift further and further away from a consciousness of God. Dependence on God used to be automatic for many of our foreparents. Church on Sundays, prayer, praise, and worship used to be a societal norm. That is no longer the case. God's name has faded into the background in our current generation. But the reunion is coming up!

GOD HELPS US BY REFRESHING OUR MEMORIES.

It had been a long time since Moses had been in Egypt. Many of them would not know Moses.

And those who knew Moses, would also remember his past actions, such as killing the Egyptian and leaving the country. Maybe many held that against him. If he suddenly showed up to declare the word of God to them, some of them probably wouldn't want to hear or believe him.

Moses asks God, "Who am I that I should go to Pharaoh and bring the Israelites out of Egypt?" (Exodus 3:11).

It's perfectly logical that Moses needed to establish his own credentials. If Moses went in his own name, he would not have credibility because his name would not be held in high regard in Egypt. He needed a name above his name that would give him authority. The only way Moses would be successful in his ministry is if he had his name attached to God's name.

GOD'S NAME IS ABOVE OUR NAME.

Today, everything is about branding. Branding is purposeful differentiation. A brand will get you noticed. A great brand becomes synonymous with your being. Nike now means "Just Do It." For Christians, the only brand that really makes a difference is the name of God! The name of Christ gives the church its authority.

God's name would redeem Moses' name. Perhaps you are in need of God's name for you. Your name is healed, purified, and redeemed by His name.

In Hebrew culture, names reflect essence. If you knew someone's name, you would know something of their nature. The Bible is filled with different names of God and the different aspects of His nature. Here is a sampling:

Hebrew Names of God	Translation	Scripture Source
El Elyon	God most high	Genesis 14
El Roi	the God who sees	Genesis 16
El Shaddai	God Almighty	Genesis 17
El Olam	the Eternal God	Genesis 21
Jehovah-Jireh	the Lord provides	Genesis 22

The names say something about who God is and what God will do. If the people knew this God's name, they would know what they could count on this God for. If He is called *Jehovah-rophe*, we know we can count on Him for healing. If He is called *Jehovah-shalom*, we know we can count on Him for peace.

God did not allow Joseph and Mary to name their son (Matthew 1:21-23). His angel told them to call Him "Jesus" ("Jehovah saves") because He would save people from their sins. The angel also told them to call Him "Emmanuel," or "God with us!"

GOD REAFFIRMS HIS RELEVANCE.

Moses knew that the Israelites might know God as the God of their ancestors. However, for them to ask now what God's name is, may not be a question of identity. It may be a question of relevance. The Israelites had heard the stories of who God had been for Abraham (the father of the Jewish nation—Genesis 11-25), Isaac (Abraham's son—Genesis 21-35), and Jacob/Israel (Isaac's son—Genesis 25-50). But now the Israelites were dealing with situations that their forefathers never had to deal with.

To ask what God's name was, was to ask who God would be in that new situation. Their issue was divine relevance. Was the God of Abraham still relevant—right now? They could praise the God who blessed Abraham and Sarah with generations of children when they were as "good as dead." They could praise the God who enabled Isaac and Rebekah to have twin boys in their advanced age. They could praise the God who watched over Jacob as he traversed the rugged terrain of this existence.

But now the Israelites were dealing with their own issues—bondage, cruelty, and injustice. Who was the God of their challenges?

Is God still relevant? This is the question for today's generation. The socialist revolutionary, Vladimir Lenin, said that God would die with the grandmothers. The German philosopher, Friedrich Nietzsche, declared that God is already dead.

African Americans saw who God was in slavery and in the Civil Rights movement. Where is God now?

Maybe the Lord delivered you from addiction fifteen years ago. Maybe you saw who God was in your life twenty years ago. But maybe, right now, you are facing a new challenge, a new Egypt.

We live in a world where technology and communication change daily, where human life is not valued, and people kill other people because of misperceived differences. Migrants and refugees trying to find a better life are suffering unimaginably in Europe—and in America. Is God still relevant?

Moses raises this question and God answers. We can imagine how it may have taken God a little time to answer. God probably thought within His own mind: "Let's see, Moses, you want to know my name? Where do I begin? I'm not sure you have time to hear everything I could say about my name. I don't know if your limited mind can fathom the ineffable mystery of the fullness of my identity. I'm struggling to answer your question, Moses, in a way that would make sense to you and fit who I am. People have tried to name me over the centuries—the unmoved mover, first cause, mysterium tremendum ("awe inspiring mystery"), numinous. I could go on for eternity, but you don't have that. The only conclusion I can come to is that 'I am who I am.' Just tell the people that: 'I am who I am.' Tell them that 'I AM' sent you."

God's response is strange. He doesn't give a proper name. Instead, He gives a statement about His being. However, when God reveals this about His name and nature, it's clear that He wants to convey a specific reason to count on Him to Moses and the Israelites in need of freedom. Something connected with His name will bless them in their present context.

GOD IS SUFFICIENT: EVERYTHING THAT IS NEEDED IS FOUND IN THE GREAT "I AM."

In Egypt, the Israelites were exposed to a multitude of Egyptian gods. There was a god for rain, fertility, fire—you name it. If you wanted healthy crops, you would pray to one god. If you wanted long life, you would pray to another god.

When God says to Moses, "I am who I am" (Exodus 3:14), He means that He is not the God of just *anything*, He is the God of *everything*. The sum of who God is is found in the great "I AM."

The late Dr. E. K. Bailey tells the story of a man who went into a Mercedes-Benz dealership to buy a new car with cash. The salesperson shows him the car, and the man is poised to buy this car with cash. However, the man has one question. He wants to know what the horsepower of the car is. For some reason, the salesperson did not know; it wasn't listed anywhere. The salesperson got on the phone and called the manufacturer and asked them what the horsepower was. The representative answered the salesperson with one word: "sufficient." In other words, whatever power was needed was underneath the hood.

Moses knew that the Israelites would want to know God's horsepower. And God says "sufficient." "I AM" means "enough." As a matter of fact, He is more than enough! Whatever the Israelites needed to reach their destiny, God would be sufficient. Moses needed to know this as well as the people. Moses' first objection was "Who am I?" God corrects his objection with the statement, "I AM." The void created by "Who am I?" is filled with the fullness of "I AM."

"I AM" is sufficient for Moses, the Israelites, and us today.

GOD IS ALWAYS A RIGHT NOW GOD.

Past, present, and future are time concepts and categories for human beings. God does not operate with those concepts or differentiations of time. God just is. Who God is is who God has been, and who God has been is who God will be. We can count on God being who God has been. If God has been a miracle worker, God *will be* a miracle worker. If God has been a liberator, God *will be* a liberator. If God has been a provider, God *will be* a provider.

The name "I AM" conveys God's eternity. This may be the heart of the matter. If anyone wonders whether God is a right now God or whether He is relevant to a new challenge, His name answers that question. God lives in the eternal now—"I AM."

God's name never needs to be upgraded. His power never needs to be improved. His grace can't be made any better. You can count on God now, the same way Moses and the Israelites counted on God in Exodus. No matter how many features the current iPhone has, something better is coming out soon. But, when it comes to God, there is nothing better. God is always a right now God.

GOD IS ABLE TO LIVE UP TO HIS NAME.

Because the Israelites had been exposed to the Egyptian gods, they may have thought that this God, in whose name Moses would come, was just another god among the other gods. The yeast of polytheism may have influenced their thinking. To say "I AM" is a statement of exclusivity. When God declares what He is, He is simultaneously declaring what everyone else is not.

This is why Jesus echoed His father in His own "I am" statements. When Jesus says, "I am...," He is also saying that no one else *is*. Like God, as God, He is on a plane all by Himself.

"I am the bread of life. He who comes to Me shall never hunger, and he who believes in Me shall never thirst" (John 6:35)

"I am the gate; whoever enters through me will be saved. They will come in and go out, and find pasture." (John 10:9)

"I am the good shepherd. The good shepherd lays down his life for the sheep. (John 10:11)

"I am the way and the truth and the life. No one comes to the Father except through me." (John 14:6)

"I am the vine; you are the branches. If you remain in me and I in you, you will bear much fruit; apart from me you can do nothing." (John 15:5)

"I am the light of the world. Whoever follows me will never walk in darkness, but will have the light of life." (John 8:12)

"I am the resurrection and the life. The one who believes in me will live, even though they die; and whoever lives by believing in me will never die. Do you believe this? (John 11:25–26)

The Israelites needed to know whom to look to in their bondage. God clarified the fact that He was their exclusive help. In trouble and adversity, when it comes to whom you ought to look, don't be confused—look to God!

OUR GOD IS A GOD OF ACTION.

When God says His name is "I AM," He is using the first-person plural of the verb "to be." The root of God's name is a verb. The root for Yahweh (YHWH, the four-letter biblical name of God) is the verb "to be." At the heart of the matter, God is a verb.

The Israelites who were in bondage needed conviction to awaken their courage and convert their despair into confidence. God tells them (and us today) that He will not sit on the sideline of life watching people go through their time of enslavement. God is going to act on their behalf. He was not like the Egyptian gods who had mouths but could not speak, who had ears but could not hear the cries of the people, and who had hands but could not reach out to help.

Our God is a God who steps into history. Our God is a God of action.

For God so loved the world that he gave his one and only Son, that whoever believes in him shall not perish but have eternal life. (John 3:16)

What did God do? Did He take a meeting to analyze the data? Did He form a caucus to make sure His law would pass? No. He *GAVE.*

God tells Moses *to go*—go home, return to his people, and keep going down the path to God's purpose for his life.

"So now, go. I am sending you to Pharaoh to bring my people the Israelites out of Egypt." (Exodus 3:10)

And, just as He calls Moses into action, He calls *us* into action.

God's name connotes sufficiency, supremacy, activity, and eternity. This is a lot for God to live up to, but God is able to live up to His name.

Are you ready to live up to *your* name in His name?

KEY POINTS

- We often end up in situations in our lives in which we settle for less than the purpose established for us by ourselves and by God.

- By speaking to us through His Spirit, God often reintroduces Himself to us.

- Because of God's immensity, we can only comprehend who He is through the attributes He reveals to us in His Word, and those attributes reflect His relevance in defining our own purpose.

- God's name, the great "I AM," reminds us that He is all-sufficient; He will help us identify our purpose and chart a course of action for our lives.

REFLECT ON THE SCRIPTURE

God said to Moses, "I AM who I AM. This is what you are to say to the Israelites: 'I AM has sent me to you.'" (Exodus 3:14)

1.   How does God resurrect a sense of purpose in Moses after 40 years of shepherding in the wilderness?

2.   Review Exodus 3:14–15. With what aspect(s) of God do you identify?

3.   In revealing Himself as the great "I AM," how do God's power, presence, and provision relate to your own quest to discover God's purpose—For you? For your family? For our nation? For the world?

4.   In the Hebrew culture, a name was given to a new member of the family to acknowledge some unique characteristic of the child, a reflection of family traits, or an expectation of future accomplishments. If you had to rename yourself, what might that name be?

5.   Examine each of the "I AM" verses on pages 6–7. What does each say to you right now at this point on your path to purpose?

REFLECT ON YOUR JOURNEY

1. Think about the times in your life when you have settled for less than what satisfies you. What were they? Why did you settle?

2. When have you felt the need to be introduced or reintroduced to God?

3. Where has God shown Himself to you or refreshed your memories of Him?

4. When have you asked God, "Who am I...?" What was His answer?

5. What is God's call to action in your life right now?

PRAYER FOR THE JOURNEY

Heavenly Father, incline our hearts, our minds, and our spirits to hear You as You speak to us about who You are—and who You expect us to be. As we travel along this road of purpose, help us to be open to understanding Your character in shaping and nurturing the plans You have for our lives. We recognize you as the great I AM and ask that You empower us to be all that You want us to be. Help us to never settle for less than what You desire for us, and help us to lean upon Your total sufficiency to complete our journey of purpose. Thank you for what You have already done in our lives. We pray that You will guide, direct, and support us in this continuing pilgrimage in Jesus' name. Amen.

CHAPTER 3

ON THE OTHER SIDE OF CHOICE

In Exodus Chapter 4, Moses continues his burning bush conversation with God. After getting the assignment to return to Egypt and lead the Israelites out of bondage, Moses—understandably—has some issues. He realizes that he is no match for the God-given task. His purpose is so much larger than he is. At this point, Moses does not understand that the assignment isn't about *him*. He also doesn't comprehend that God rarely provides a purpose smaller than what He can help you accomplish.

A God-given purpose is always bigger than you because God intends to work *through* you to accomplish His plan for you. But we tend to limit ourselves—with fear, uncertainty, questions, and walls.

The impala is an amazing animal. It can jump to a height of more than 10 feet and cover a distance greater than 30 feet. Yet, if you visit a zoo, these magnificent creatures can be kept in an enclosure with only a 3-foot wall. The reason for this is that the impala will not jump if it cannot see where its feet will land. So, it ends up captive to a situation from which it could be freed if only it took the risk of a single leap.

God doesn't always show us where we are going to end up, but somewhere along the way He will call us to leap. We get stuck in life because we can't see where our feet are going to land. We gaze at purpose and possibility over what is, in reality, a relatively small obstacle. We can see a whole world outside of the enclosure, but we will not jump. The monotonous security of the enclosure is more appealing to us than the risk of life beyond it.

Think about where you might be on your journey to purpose if you weren't worried about where your feet would land as you read Exodus Chapter 4.

WE ALL WANT TO KNOW WHAT'S ON THE OTHER SIDE.

In a very real sense, the Lord was calling Moses to jump. Moses had been stuck behind the enclosure of shepherding. There was nothing wrong with shepherding, but God was now purposing more for Moses. And Moses is questioning that purpose.

Moses answered, "What if they do not believe me or listen to me and say, 'The Lord did not appear to you'?"

Then the Lord said to him, "What is that in your hand?"

"A staff," he replied.

The Lord said, "Throw it on the ground."

Moses threw it on the ground and it became a snake, and he ran from it. Then the Lord said to him, "Reach out your hand and take it by the tail." So Moses reached out and took hold of the snake and it turned back into a staff in his hand. "This," said the Lord, "is so that they may believe that the Lord, the God of their fathers—the God of Abraham, the God of Isaac and the God of Jacob—has appeared to you."

Then the Lord said, "Put your hand inside your cloak." So Moses put his hand into his cloak, and when he took it out, the skin was leprous—it had become as white as snow.

"Now put it back into your cloak," he said. So Moses put his hand back into his cloak, and when he took it out, it was restored, like the rest of his flesh.

Then the Lord said, "If they do not believe you or pay attention to the first sign, they may believe the second. But if they do not believe these two signs or listen to you, take some water from the

Nile and pour it on the dry ground. The water you take from the river will become blood on the ground." (Exodus 4:1–8)

Moses goes back and forth with God, who basically says, "You do the work, and leave the results to me." This is an important lesson to keep in mind: Our role is the work; God's role is the results.

OBEDIENCE ACTIVATES GOD'S PURPOSE AND PLAN.

Moses is a reluctant liberator. He says, "I have a speech impediment. I can't even say, 'Let my people go.'" And God responds.

The Lord said to him, "Who gave human beings their mouths? Who makes them deaf or mute? Who gives them sight or makes them blind? Is it not I, the Lord? Now go; I will help you speak and will teach you what to say." (Exodus 4:9)

God factored in Moses' deficiencies when He gave him the assignment. What better assurances to have than God's promises of divine assistance and teaching?

But Moses backs away from the fence, saying, "Pardon your servant, Lord. Please send someone else" (Exodus 4:13). Like the impala, Moses will not leap because he cannot see where he will land.

God was hoping for a running leap. Instead, Moses is trying to run the other way. God tells him that He will not send anybody else. However, He partners Moses with his brother Aaron.

"You shall speak to him and put words in his mouth; I will help both of you speak and will teach you what to do. He will speak to the people for you, and it will be as if he were your mouth and as if you were God to him." (Exodus 4:15–16)

Then some time elapses. We aren't sure how long Moses takes to think about his purpose.

Then Moses went back to Jethro his father-in-law and said to him, "Let me return to my own people in Egypt to see if any of them are still alive."

Jethro said, "Go, and I wish you well." (Exodus 4:18)

Moses has embraced his purpose. There is no record of how he feels, only a record of his choice. How he feels is less important than his choice. Moses had to choose; God wasn't going to send anyone else. It had to be him.

At some point, we all just have to make a choice—no more negotiation, discussion, or debate. Prayer time is over. Therapy is over. Analysis is over. You can't stay behind the fence forever. You just have to choose—and one of those choices is to go in the direction God is leading you. Will you stay in the enclosure or will you leap?

PURPOSE BEGINS WITH A CHOICE.

Fundamentally, life is about choice. God can work with choice; God can't do much with indecision. The prophet Joshua posed a similar question to the Israelites once they were freed and had become a nation: "...choose you this day whom you will serve..." (Joshua 24:15).

"Now fear the Lord and serve him with all faithfulness. Throw away the gods your ancestors worshiped beyond the Euphrates River and in Egypt, and serve the Lord. But if serving the Lord seems undesirable to you, then choose for yourselves this day whom you will serve, whether the gods your ancestors served beyond the Euphrates, or the gods of the Amorites, in whose land you are living. But as for me and my household, we will serve the Lord."

Then the people answered, "Far be it from us to forsake the Lord to serve other gods! It was the Lord our God himself who brought us and our parents up out of Egypt, from that land of slavery, and performed those great signs before our eyes. He protected us on our entire journey and among all the nations through which we traveled. And the Lord drove out before us all the nations, including the Amorites, who lived in the land. We too will serve the Lord, because he is our God."

Joshua said to the people, "You are not able to serve the Lord. He is a holy God; he is a jealous God. He will not forgive your rebellion and your sins. If you forsake the Lord and serve foreign gods, he will turn and bring disaster on you and make an end of you, after he has been good to you."

But the people said to Joshua, "No! We will serve the Lord."

Then Joshua said, "You are witnesses against yourselves that you have chosen to serve the Lord."

"Yes, we are witnesses," they replied.

"Now then," said Joshua, "throw away the foreign gods that are among you and yield your hearts to the Lord, the God of Israel."

And the people said to Joshua, "We will serve the Lord our God and obey him." (Joshua 24:14–24)

Just like the future Israelites will profess, Moses, in his burning bush conversation with God, chooses to obey God's purpose for him. On the other side of his choice, before he can leave, he has to speak to his father-in-law, Jethro. No matter how important Moses' assignment is, he still has to deal with his elders in the right way. Jethro fed, clothed, housed, employed, and made Moses a part of his family when Moses was jobless and broke. Moses needed to leave in the right way.

If you ever need to leave the house of your provider (young folks in particular), try to leave in a way that you can come back. Show respect to those who have enabled you along your journey to purpose. You never know when you might have to journey back to Jethro's house.

If Moses had been accepted into the Midianite nation, he would need permission to withdraw himself from the tribal head. Moses knew that nations and tribes were anxious to keep up their numbers. They frowned on the desertion of even one member. He probably assumed (correctly) that this was not going to be an easy conversation. His nerves are on edge as he approaches Jethro.

PEOPLE WHO HAVE NOT SEEN THE BURNING BUSH WON'T ALWAYS UNDERSTAND THE PURPOSE.

When Moses tells Jethro that he wants to go to Egypt to see if any of his people are still alive, he does not tell him the whole story (Exodus 4:18). He knew that you have to be careful who you share your purpose with. The last thing you need after your burning bush moment is for people who haven't seen the bush to raise doubt and opposition in your mind.

Moses did not know if Jethro and his present situation were going to be willing to let him go. Moses could have thwarted his own purpose by giving up at this point. He could have seen this potential obstacle of having to deal with Jethro as a deal breaker, but he chooses to leap and speak to Jethro anyway.

> *Then Moses went back to Jethro his father-in-law and said to him, "Let me return to my own people in Egypt to see if any of them are still alive."*
>
> *Jethro said, "Go, and I wish you well." (Exodus 4:18)*

Not only does Jethro give him permission, but he bestows a blessing. Moses is granted both permission and peace.

SOMETIMES, WHAT WE THINK IS GOING TO BE AN OBSTACLE, ENDS UP BEING A BLESSING.

Right after Moses' conversation with Jethro, God speaks to him.

Now, remember, Moses was on the "most wanted" list for the murder of the Egyptian. There were those, including the king, who sought Moses' life. Going back to Egypt, for Moses, was going to be complicated, and this thought must have entered his mind. However, there is no record of him mentioning it to God.

Like Moses, we don't need to voice everything to God; God can read our thoughts. God knows our personalities, our mindsets, and our situations. As we are on the pilgrimage to actualizing our purpose, God knows when we need to hear a word—His Word.

WHEN GOD'S HAND IS ON YOU, YOU CAN OUTLIVE YOUR STORM.

God tells Moses that everyone who intended to kill him in Egypt is now dead (Exodus 4:19). The people who had meant to destroy Moses had died off. This was Moses' storm. Because of his time in Midian and God's watchful eye, Moses outlived his storm. With God, you, too, can outlive whoever or whatever is trying to destroy you.

The late Dr. Caesar Clark preached a sermon titled "The Worms Got Him." It was based on Acts 12 in which Herod had killed James and attempted to kill Peter to stop the progress of the Word of God.

Immediately, because Herod did not give praise to God, an angel of the Lord struck him down, and he was eaten by worms and died.

But the word of God continued to spread and flourish. (Acts 12:23-24)

You don't have to fight all of your opposition. You don't have to try to destroy those who aimed to destroy you. The worms will get them! What Moses thought was going to be an issue was no issue at all. On the other side of Moses' choice came the absence of the adversary.

THE JOURNEY TO PURPOSE CAN BE LONELY; GOD CAN SEND CONSOLATION IN THE DESERT!

When Moses first left for Egypt, he took his wife Zipporah and their two sons with him. However, at some point, Moses sent them back.

After Moses had sent away his wife Zipporah, his father-in-law Jethro received her and her two sons. (Exodus 18:2-3)

We don't know why. But, whatever the case, Moses ended up being alone for some time. When walking into your purpose, not everyone can travel with you toward what God has purposed for you. There are times when you intentionally choose solitude.

During Moses' journey, God sent his brother, Aaron, to meet him in the desert.

The Lord said to Aaron, "Go into the wilderness to meet Moses." So he met Moses at the mountain of God and kissed him. Then Moses told Aaron everything the Lord had sent him to say, and also about all the signs he had commanded him to perform. (Exodus 4:27-28)

Maybe you've been in the desert of loneliness or heartbreak. Maybe there have been people who God used to encourage you, without them even knowing how close you were to giving up. Maybe God sent a card, e-mail, or text your way— somebody who offered you consolation in the desert. God knows what we need when we need it.

GOD CAN POSITION PEOPLE IN YOUR LIFE TO HELP YOU ON YOUR JOURNEY TO PURPOSE.

Aaron was not there just for Moses' consolation; he was also there to help Moses accomplish his purpose. God sends certain people to your life to help you get where He's guiding you to go.

One afternoon in October 1954, a twelve-year-old, Cassius Clay rode his brand-new bicycle to the Columbia Auditorium to get free popcorn and ice cream. Cassius left his red and white Schwinn bike outside, but when he came back, the bike was gone. Someone had stolen it. Cassius burst into tears. Someone told him that there was an old, white-haired policeman in the basement of a building that had a boxing gym. Young Cassius, fuming with hurt and anger, found the officer, Joe Martin. When Cassius said, "Someone took my new bike and, when I find them, I'm going to beat them up." Joe Martin just laughed at him and said, "Before you can beat them up, you first need to learn how to fight." It was Joe Martin who introduced Cassius Clay (later known as Mohammed Ali) to the punching bag, and the rest is history.

God arranges people to meet you along the way who you didn't even plan to meet. Where would Cassius Clay have been had Joe Martin not been positioned where he was? Where would Moses have been if Aaron had not met him in the desert? Many of us have a Joe Martin or an Aaron whom we need to thank—and for whom we need to thank God.

WORSHIP IS STILL POSSIBLE WHILE WE'RE IN BONDAGE IN EGYPT.

Not long after arriving in Egypt, Moses and Aaron went to the community of elders. Their cooperation was going to be very important. These were people who formerly would not have listened to Moses. Many did not know who Moses was, and the ones who knew him were very aware of his past deeds. But because God was involved, their ears were opened.

Moses and Aaron brought together all the elders of the Israelites, and Aaron told them everything the Lord had said to Moses. He also performed the signs before the people, and they believed. And when they heard that the Lord was concerned about them and had seen their misery, they bowed down and worshiped. (Exodus 4:27–31)

Not only did they believe what was said and seen, they worshipped *because* of it. The elders were given a Word from God. They praised God based on the promise of what He was going to do. They were still in bondage, but they were able to worship!

YOU DON'T KNOW WHAT'S ON THE OTHER SIDE OF CHOICE UNTIL YOU'RE ON THE OTHER SIDE OF CHOICE.

On the other side of choice, Moses was blessed with the permission of his patriarch, the absence of his adversaries, the bond of brotherhood, and the cooperation of the community. It would have been easy for Moses to talk himself out of going to Egypt based on all of these hurdles, these fences. It is tempting for us to talk ourselves out of desires, dreams, and purpose based on real and anticipated obstacles. It is so tempting to stay within the enclosures because of what we think is on the other side.

God has a way of dealing with real and anticipated obstacles and our subsequent anxieties. God dealt with all of Moses' anxieties—talking with Jethro, returning to Egypt, being alone in the desert, and facing the Israelite elders. There are no obstacles bigger than God!

Moses never would have discovered that all of his worries would be dealt with until he made the choice to be true to his purpose. On the other side of choice, God is already active. Moses did not have all the information. All he has is a promise and a purpose. But he chooses God's way anyway.

Now, it's good not to try to choose a way forward before God gives us a direction. But after you sense His direction, it's time to go to Egypt. To walk by faith is to move with limited information and leap forward even when you have every non-God reason to stay. You don't know what's on the other side of choice, but God does.

Are you ready to trust God and leap?

KEY POINTS

- God is able and willing to work through us to accomplish what we cannot do on our own.

- God has an answer for every excuse.

- After discerning our purpose, we should internalize it and use wisdom in sharing it with the trusted companions who journey with us.

- We should never let potential obstacles deter us; they may not even exist.

- God is already orchestrating people, events, and circumstances to accomplish your purpose—so take the risk and leap. You may be surprised at how God has prepared a safe and fruitful landing.

REFLECT ON THE SCRIPTURE

Now the Lord had said to Moses in Midian, "Go back to Egypt, for all those who wanted to kill you are dead." (Exodus 4:19)

1. Review Exodus 4:1–8. When has God shown you signs in your life?

2. Why would you want to be cautious of who you share a "burning bush moment" with?

REFLECT ON YOUR JOURNEY

1. Where in your life are you standing behind a 3-foot fence looking out into possibility?

2. What are some of the obstacles you perceive as your fences right now?

3. What would it take for you to leap forward in your purpose?

4. Think of a time when there was a storm in your life. Where was God?

5. Who has God sent to console you in the desert?

6. Who has God positioned in your life to help you on your journey?

7. Review Exodus 4:27–31. At this point on your journey to purpose, what can you praise or thank God for?

8. In what direction is God pointing you toward now? Are you going to stay behind the fence, or are you going to choose to make a leap of faith, in spite of what's on the other side?

PRAYER FOR THE JOURNEY

All-knowing and all-loving God, we are grateful for the challenge to move forward. Forgive us for not always taking the risk to leap. God, we often stay where we are until we get assurance of where You are taking us. We ask for the strength to trust Your heart even when we cannot trace Your hand. In this moment, we surrender our need to know. In Jesus' name. Amen.

CHAPTER 4

WHEN IT GOES FROM BAD TO WORSE

At the end of Exodus Chapter 4, things were going pretty well for Moses. God provided him with a purpose, a partner (his brother, Aaron), and a blessing from the head of the household (his father-in-law, Jethro). Most of all, Moses has God with him. Upon arriving in Egypt, Moses performed miraculous signs before the Israelite elders—his staff was transformed into a snake and his cloak both caused and restored leprosy—and the elders believed that God, through Moses, would rescue them (Exodus 4:1-7, 30-31). All of Moses' past enemies were now dead, so what's left to stop him from leading his people to the place that God had purposed for them, the Promised Land?

Read Exodus Chapters 5 and 6 to find out.

SOMETIMES YOU HAVE TO ENDURE A SEASON OF DISTRESS AND GRIEF ON THE JOURNEY.

Moses and Aaron go to the new king of Egypt, but the new Pharaoh is not as receptive as they had hoped.

Afterward Moses and Aaron went to Pharaoh and said, "This is what the Lord, the God of Israel, says: 'Let my people go, so that they may hold a festival to me in the wilderness.'"

Pharaoh said, "Who is the Lord, that I should obey him and let Israel go? I do not know the Lord and I will not let Israel go." (Exodus 5:1–2)

In the face of this staunch opposition, Moses and Aaron convey that God wants the entire nation of Israel to worship God in the desert or dire consequences will befall them.

Then they said, "The God of the Hebrews has met with us. Now let us take a three-day journey into the wilderness to offer sacrifices to the Lord our God, or he may strike us with plagues or with the sword."

But the king of Egypt said, "Moses and Aaron, why are you taking the people away from their labor? Get back to your work!" Then Pharaoh said, "Look, the people of the land are now numerous, and you are stopping them from working." (Exodus 5:3–5)

It's now clear that evil is not going to give up without a fight.

Pharaoh then commands that the work be made harder for the Israelites but expects the same productivity despite the new burdens placed upon them. The plight of the Israelites grows darker and harsher.

That same day Pharaoh gave this order to the slave drivers and overseers in charge of the people: "You are no longer to supply the people with straw for making bricks; let them go and gather their own straw. But require them to make the same number of bricks as before; don't reduce the quota. They are lazy; that is why they are crying out, 'Let us go and sacrifice to our God.' Make the work harder for the people so that they keep working and pay no attention to lies." (Exodus 5:6-9)

At first, the Israelite overseers attempt to appeal to Pharaoh, but they are immediately insulted and ordered to get back to work.

Pharaoh said, "Lazy, that's what you are— lazy! That is why you keep saying, 'Let us go and sacrifice to the Lord.' Now get to work. You will not be given any straw, yet you must produce your full quota of bricks." (Exodus 4:17-18)

During the civil rights movement, Dr. Martin Luther King, Jr. and members of the Southern Christian Leadership Conference were often referred to as agitators—people who would go into segregated cities and stir up trouble. And, many times, this complaint came from fellow African Americans who had become resigned to and accepted their oppression or were afraid to do anything about it. Likewise, the Israelite overseers go to Moses and Aaron and accuse them of being agitators.

> *The Israelite overseers realized they were in trouble when they were told, "You are not to reduce the number of bricks required of you for each day." When they left Pharaoh, they found Moses and Aaron waiting to meet them, and they said, "May the Lord look on you and judge you! You have made us obnoxious to Pharaoh and his officials and have put a sword in their hand to kill us." (Exodus 4:19–21)*

Moses is completely distraught because it's true that he has made the Israelites' circumstances far worse than they were before. And now he is publicly blamed for the tightening of the grip of oppression. What would you do in a time like this?

In his painful season of distress and grief, at least Moses knows where to go. It's one thing to have a tough season. It's another thing to have a tough season and not know where to go. Verse 22 says "Moses *returned* to the Lord..." Had Moses drifted away from God? Sometimes devotion wanes in the season of prosperity and favor. Perhaps Moses' feet had strayed from the pathway of devotion and commitment. He "returned to the Lord." You, too, can return to God amid the pain and disappointment on your journey.

I'M IN THE MESS YOU GOT ME INTO.

Plans are not working out the way Moses thought they would. In fact, things had actually been a lot better before he obeyed God. Life, tending sheep in the wasteland, had been good. He had been secure and peaceful. His people were in bondage, but at least they seemed to have adjusted to it. Now that God is involved, things are chaotic, and it seems as if the plight of Moses and his people goes from bad to worse. So, Moses complains to God.

Moses returned to the Lord and said, "Why, Lord, why have you brought trouble on this people? Is this why you sent me? Ever since I went to Pharaoh to speak in your name, he has brought trouble on this people, and you have not rescued your people at all." (Exodus 5:22–23)

In other words, Moses is saying, "God, I'm in the mess that *You* got me into. My faithfulness to You has led me into trouble. Is this what You have planned for me?"

It is true that sometimes, even with God's involvement in your situation, things can go from bad to worse. There are some messes we get ourselves into, some that other people get us into, some that the devil gets us into, and then some that God gets us into.

Moses is now living in purpose—he goes to tell Pharaoh to let the people go. But Moses discovers that living in purpose is not always easy. Evil has to be overcome along the way. Obstacles have to be dealt with along the way. Just because you are going in the direction God wants you to go does not mean there won't be any hurdles. However, you can't let the existence of failures, obstacles, and trouble make you think that you are not on the right path.

When things go from bad to worse, even when you seem to be walking in the direction God wanted you to go, what do you do? How do you stay on the path to purpose? God's response to Moses gives us some clues.

Then the Lord said to Moses, "Now you will see what I will do to Pharaoh: Because of my mighty hand he will let them go; because of my mighty hand he will drive them out of his country." (Exodus 6:1)

Unlike the time when Moses asked God to choose anyone else but him to lead the people out of Egypt, God isn't mad at Moses. He doesn't chastise Moses for having the audacity to complain to and even blame God for his predicament. God can handle Moses' plaintive prayer and may even appreciate it. At least Moses is being honest!

What God can't handle is when we are dishonest in our expressions of prayers. Prayer is the emptying of the content of the soul. Sometimes that content is not so pretty, but God can handle our deepest frustrations. There are days that you are not "fine," when you don't feel blessed. It's alright to tell God how you feel about those days.

After Moses expresses his honest feelings, God starts talking. Now, we don't know how long it took God to speak. It's difficult to gauge the timing from the word "Then" in Exodus 6:1. It could have been immediately; it could have taken some time. Whatever the case, God speaks.

It's interesting that there is no record of God saying anything in Exodus Chapter 5. Moses, Aaron, Pharaoh, the Egyptian slave drivers and Israelite overseers speak. Everyone in this chapter is talking, except for God. While the grip of evil tightens and the situation grows worse, God is silent.

71

There are chapters in our lives during which God is silent, times when God seems to be on the sidelines watching things go quickly downhill. Sometimes God sits back and allows your physician, lawyer, friends, and family to offer their words of wisdom. Then, out of nowhere, God speaks. In your darkest hour, the word of God will pierce your hardened despair. You have to open your ears and eyes for His alternative word.

WHEN LIFE GOES FROM BAD TO WORSE, STAY OPEN TO GOD'S WORD.

God can speak in a variety of ways. Be open to however God might speak to you.

Not long ago, I was having a tough week. I was trying to figure out how some unexpected financial crises were going to work out. I had been praying all week. I needed God to say something about how I was going to pay for this and then pay for that. College tuition was staring me straight in the face. All week, God had not said anything to me. I watched a television preacher (which I rarely do) looking for a word. I sat out on my sister's deck and read my Bible looking for a word. I checked my phone for an inspirational text. Nothing.

In frustration, I stared down at the ground and saw ants carrying crumbs of food which had fallen from the night before. I gazed up into the trees and saw two squirrels gathering walnuts to store for the winter. I looked across the street and saw Canadian geese eating apples that had fallen from the apple trees. In the midst of my anxiety about some circumstances which seemed to have gone from bad to worse, I heard a word from God: "'Look at the birds of the air; they do not sow or reap or store away in barns, and yet your heavenly Father feeds them' (Matthew 6:26). I will take care of you!"

Even in despair, be open for the alternative word of God, especially if it comes through some unorthodox channels.

KEEP TRUSTING GOD'S PURPOSE.

After Moses tells Pharaoh to let the people go, Pharaoh doubles down on his oppression of the Israelites. But life was contradicting what God promised—that He would set the Israelites free. Moses doesn't know that Pharaoh's actions are actually serving the purpose of God.

God says to Moses, "Now you will see..." (Exodus 6:1). The tightening of the oppressor's grip would allow Moses to see just how great and mighty God is. Circumstances that appear to oppose God's purpose may actually be fulfilling God's plan.

In the New Testament, Jesus is born to be the Savior and rescue the people yet again: "For the Son of Man came to seek and to save the lost" (Luke 19:10). But, in the minds of His followers, Jesus' death on the cross contradicts the purposes of God. The twelve best students of Jesus, the disciples, did not know that the cross was a part of the plan which would serve the purpose of accomplishing salvation. Sometimes the worst thing that could happen is actually serving the purposes of God. We don't learn that the cross serves God's purposes until after the resurrection. That's why you have to hang in there even when things go from bad to worse. Sunday helps make sense of some Fridays. On some of our "Fridays," God may allow some trouble close enough to us so that we will have front row seats to the display of His great power. God may keep certain enemies close enough to you so that you can see their defeat. Friday is hellish, but Sunday is coming!

On Moses' particular "Friday," God allows the cards to be stacked against Moses and the people in order for them to "see." God wants them to see how the mighty arm of God will overpower the fist of Pharaoh. The hand of righteousness will ultimately crush the hand of oppression.

"Therefore, say to the Israelites: 'I am the Lord, and I will bring you out from under the yoke of the Egyptians. I will free you from being slaves to them, and I will redeem you with an outstretched arm and with mighty acts of judgment. I will take you as my own people, and I will be your God. Then you will know that I am the Lord your God, who brought you out from under the yoke of the Egyptians. And I will bring you to the land I swore with uplifted hand to give to Abraham, to Isaac and to Jacob. I will give it to you as a possession. I am the Lord.'" (Exodus 6:6–8)

Every now and then, God can make it so that whatever has you will get sick of you and let you go. The story of 10-year-old Willie Myrick is a perfect example. In April 2014, Willie was kidnapped from his driveway in Atlanta, Georgia. The suspect lured him into the car with cash, grabbed him, and locked him in the car. In the car, young Willie started singing his favorite gospel song, "Every Praise Is to Our God." He kept singing it until he got on his abductor's last nerve, and the kidnapper told him to get out of the car! God can make it so that you get on the enemy's nerve to the point that whatever has you has to let you go.

God is telling Moses that His purposes are still intact. God just needs Moses to stick with His game plan. Apparent failure isn't going to change the game plan. God's game plan is for Moses and Aaron to keep talking to Pharaoh. That does not change just because they fail the first time! Even in failure, you can trust that God's purpose remains intact!

KEEP GOD'S CHARACTER IN MIND.

The critical question that Pharaoh asks after being challenged by Moses and Aaron is "Who is the Lord?" This question is at the center of the entire narrative. In answer to Moses, God says, "I am who I AM" (Exodus 3:14) and reminds Moses of His name. When things go from bad to worse, we sometimes forget what God's name is. Bad health, rocky relationships, and financial hardships can make you forget God's name. In those times, we don't need new revelation; we just need to be reminded who God is. We need to be reminded that God is our refuge and our strength.

The Lord is my shepherd; I shall not want. (Psalm 23:1, King James Version)

The Lord is my rock, my fortress and my deliverer; my God is my rock, in whom I take refuge, my shield and the horn of my salvation, my stronghold. (Psalm 18:2)

In the worst of times, everybody looks for a new revelation when we might just need a reminder.

God tells Moses that the founding fathers—Abraham, Isaac, and Jacob/Israel—knew God's name, but did not really know what that name meant because they had not seen that name in action.

God also said to Moses, "I am the Lord. I appeared to Abraham, to Isaac and to Jacob as God Almighty, but by my name the Lord I did not make myself fully known to them. (Exodus 6:2-3)

Moses and the Israelites were going to know God's name *and* know what it means. Remember that the name of God is known by what God does. They are about to see that name in action.

Some people know the name 'Jesus,' but because they have not embraced Him by faith, they don't know what that name means. You won't know that His name has saving power until you have been delivered!

Moses, according to God, is going to receive the revelation of God's name, but he also receives confirmation of God's faithfulness. Even though things had gone from bad to worse, Moses could count on God because of God's covenant with Abraham. Moses and the Israelites are connected to Abraham. Therefore, God's covenant and promise extends to them.

When things go from bad to worse for you, don't give up because you don't know how close you are to deliverance! Remember who you are connected to.

For those who are led by the Spirit of God are the children of God. The Spirit you received does not make you slaves, so that you live in fear again; rather, the Spirit you received brought about your adoption to sonship. And by him we cry, "Abba, Father." The Spirit himself testifies with our spirit that we are God's children. Now if we are children, then we are heirs—heirs of God and co-heirs with Christ, if indeed we share in his sufferings in order that we may also share in his glory. (Romans 8:14–17)

Because of your connection to Christ, God will save you!

The journey to purpose includes some seasons when life can go from bad to worse. The key is being able to stay on course during those seasons by trusting in God's name.

Are you ready to know and trust in His name?

KEY POINTS

- Personal setbacks will often arise when we pursue God's purpose for us.

- It is convenient and self-serving to blame God when things do not go our way, but remember that God is ultimately in control of the results and timing of our purpose.

- When circumstances appear to contradict the accomplishment of our purpose, focus on God's Word and character; this will ensure that we remain faithful on our journey.

REFLECT ON THE SCRIPTURE

Then the Lord said to Moses, "Now you will see what I will do to Pharaoh: Because of my mighty hand he will let them go; because of my mighty hand he will drive them out of his country." (Exodus 6:1)

1. When Pharaoh commands that the work be made harder for the Israelites, how does their response reflect on their faith in God?

2. Why would the Israelites accept oppression and turn against the people who were trying to lead them out of it? When has this happened historically or in present times?

3. Were Pharaoh's actions actually serving the purpose of God? Why or why not?

REFLECT ON YOUR JOURNEY

1. Do you ever expect the same productivity of yourself despite new burdens placed on you? What can you do in this situation?

2. Do you believe that following God can make things go from bad to worse? Why?

3. How has God "messed up" your life?

4. When has God spoken an "alternative word" to you, perhaps through some unorthodox channels?

5. Where has God been when you were going through a tough season?

6. When has God's mighty hand delivered you from exile, hardship, or oppression?

7. How can you develop more faith and trust in God?

PRAYER FOR THE JOURNEY

God, we thank you for the privilege of serving You and allowing us to be a vehicle for achieving Your purpose. When we are confounded or hindered by our circumstances, help us to understand that we cannot always see the big picture. Help us to see that the impediments we face may be a part of working out Your divine plan. Lord, we look to You and place our concerns at Your feet as we recognize your power, presence and provision as Sovereign God. Lead us and guide us. Increase our faith along this journey as we follow Your will and Your way. These blessings we ask in Jesus' precious name. Amen.

CHAPTER 5

A WORD IN SEASON

Moses is trusting in God's name when he and Aaron go to Pharaoh with God's message to "let my people go." Moses might assume that his job was going to be stress-less and pain-free—especially because God had used divine favor to demolish the obstacles leading up to this audience—but it didn't work out that way. Instead of releasing the Israelites, Pharaoh commanded the slave drivers and overseers to intensify the oppression by making the slaves find their own straw to make bricks. The Israelites now blame Moses—and perhaps God—for their worsening circumstances. Moses himself is probably angry with God, fearful for his life, and doubtful about his ability to fulfill the purpose God gave him.

During our journey, we encounter seasons of blessing and seasons of trouble. When we need reassurance that God is with us during difficult times, He knows how to speak to us.

"The right word at the right time is like precious gold set in silver" (Proverbs 25:11, Contemporary English Version).

This "right word" is the Word of God.

Some of us probably would not have made it out of certain seasons had it not been for a word from someone on a similar journey or someone with past experience of the same type of season you might be in. Perhaps you have had days when God spoke directly to your season. If you heard that word in church, you might have wondered how the preacher knew what you needed to hear. It had nothing to do with the preacher; that was the Spirit of God.

During this tough season, God speaks to Moses. Read Exodus 7:1–5.

GOD KNOWS WHAT YOU NEED TO HEAR AND WHEN YOU NEED TO HEAR IT.

On the journey to purpose, sometimes we need confirmation that we are headed in the right direction. When we are trying to drive to a place we have never been, we need our navigation system to speak up and say that our destination is just ahead. We can keep going confidently when we hear that voice.

During Moses' disappointment with Pharaoh in Exodus 6, God is talking to Moses. In the beginning of Exodus 7, God is still speaking. You would think by now that Moses shouldn't need any more encouragement, that his faith should be stronger. Hadn't God spoken to Moses from the beginning? Hadn't God shown him signs and wonders? For whatever reason, Moses is not there yet, so God keeps on speaking. God doesn't deal with us based on "should" or "ought"; God deals with us based on "what is."

God has a standard that He wants Moses to meet—the standard of faith. But Moses is still struggling. The blessing is that God doesn't just deal with us at the level of *the standard*; God deals with us at the level of *our struggles*. The standard for God does not change; it is never compromised. He keeps working with us until we meet the standard. People (maybe even your family and friends) might give up on you because they think that you ought to have met the standard by now, but God will keep meeting you at the level of your struggle.

GOD GIVES MOSES (AND US) A WORD IN SEASON: THE PLAN HASN'T CHANGED.

In this season of self-doubt, God needs Moses to focus on who God has "made" Moses. The person Moses is *right now* (the man who challenges the king of Egypt) is not the same person he was before (the murderer who fled or the shepherd in the desert). God is using Moses' journey to make him into who he is now. God needs Moses to *live out* what he has been *made into*.

Then the Lord said to Moses, "See, I have made you like God to Pharaoh, and your brother Aaron will be your prophet. (Exodus 7:1)

Moses is not God, but he is God's representative. In Exodus 6:12, Moses says to God, "If the Israelites will not listen to me, why would Pharaoh listen to me, since I speak with faltering lips?" Moses knows his own inadequacies, as well as Pharaoh's obvious superiority. However, God elevates Moses over Pharaoh by saying "I have made you like God to Pharaoh" (Exodus 7:1). Because of God's elevation of Moses, Pharaoh is now subject to, or "under," him.

God's elevation overrides qualifications. We may wonder how certain people reach certain levels in life despite the fact that they don't have the perceived qualifications. Divine elevation is mysterious and doesn't always mesh with logic. God is able to elevate us above the limitations of our resume, background, race, ethnicity, and gender.

To an extent, DNA and life experiences can author how we are made. But, ultimately, God made us.

And you he made alive, when you were dead through the trespasses and sins in which you once walked, following the course of this world, following the prince of the power of the air, the spirit that is now at work in the sons of disobedience. Among these we all once lived in the passions of our flesh, following the desires of body and mind, and so we were by nature children of wrath, like the rest of mankind. But God, who is rich in mercy, out of the great love with which he loved us, even when we were dead through our trespasses, made us alive together with Christ (by grace you have been saved), and raised us up with him, and made us sit with him in the heavenly places in Christ Jesus, that in the coming ages he might show the immeasurable riches of his grace in kindness toward us in Christ Jesus. For by grace you have been saved through faith; and this is not your own doing, it is the gift of God— not because of works, lest any man should boast. For we are his workmanship, created in Christ Jesus for good works, which God prepared beforehand, that we should walk in them. (Ephesians 2:1–10)

In Midian, God finds Moses as a murderer on the run, a stuttering shepherd, and a man with limited options. There is a huge distance between how God finds Moses and what God makes of Moses. In Moses' season of self-doubt, he is still operating based on how God "found" him. God's response is to challenge Moses to focus on what God *made* him.

Sometimes there is a world of difference between how God finds some of us and what God makes us to be. We may start our journey one way, and in the course of our travels, we can be "made" by God into something else. Our choices in life either bring us closer to who God is making us or take us on a detour away from God's purpose for us. You can choose to live as what you have been made, not how you were found!

IN SOME SEASONS, GOD "CALLS YOU AGAIN" TO REAFFIRM YOUR PURPOSE.

Certain seasons of pity make us feel as if we are alone. In tough seasons, we unnecessarily cut ourselves off from our support systems. God had to remind Moses that he was not alone—that he still has Aaron and still has God.

You are to say everything I command you, and your brother Aaron is to tell Pharaoh to let the Israelites go out of his country. (Exodus 7:2)

God once again tells Moses to tell his brother Aaron to tell Pharaoh everything God says, which is ultimately, "Let my people go." This is the original plan; it hasn't changed or been altered by circumstance.

God is confirming His purpose for Moses. And God doesn't call Moses just one time; He keeps calling. In season and out of season, God can reaffirm your purpose. No matter how crazy things get or how unpredictable and unsettling life becomes, the purpose God has for you is for *you*!

GOD TELLS THE WHOLE STORY: SOMETIMES THE ROAD IS GOING TO BE OPPOSED.

God warns Moses that, although his purpose remains intact and affirmed, the opposition is real. God is honest about adversity. When God gives Moses the affirmation of his assignment, He informs him that it's not going to work as Moses anticipates!

But I will harden Pharaoh's heart, and though I multiply my signs and wonders in Egypt, he will not listen to you. (Exodus 7:3-4)

Now, it's one thing to find out that your assignment fails after you try it; it's another to hear that it's not going to work *before* you even try it. Even before Moses takes the test, he's informed that he will get an "F." Even before the game starts, he's told that he's going to lose. The assignment is doomed before it starts.

With God, there can be health, wealth, and prosperity—but that's just half the story. God tells the whole story. He doesn't hide the reality of opposition.

In the same way, Jesus also tells the whole story to His disciples:

"I have told you these things, so that in me you may have peace. In this world you will have trouble. But take heart! I have overcome the world." (John 16:33)

Jesus does not hide painful experiences or the cost of following God in the fine print. Jesus gives both sides of the story—the trouble and the turning point, the crisis and the resolution.

GOD'S GRACE CAN KEEP YOU FROM BEING WHO YOU ARE INSISTING ON BEING.

We know from Moses' first audience with the king of the land that Pharaoh is very stubborn.

Pharaoh said, "Who is the Lord, that I should obey him and let Israel go? I do not know the Lord and I will not let Israel go." (Exodus 5:2)

Pharaoh is already obstinate in his unwillingness to let the Israelites go. This is already in his character.

The heart is the source of our will and the seat of our sensitivity. A hardened heart becomes insensitive to outside influences. It becomes impervious to the voice and spirit of God. When God says, "I will harden Pharaoh's heart" (Exodus 7:3),

God is saying that He is going to allow Pharaoh to be what he already is. In fact, God says that He will intensify this characteristic in Pharaoh.

God will allow us to be who we insist on being, even if it goes against His purpose. God may not have to do much to judge us; sometimes, He just has to let us go in the direction we are insisting on going. However, God will always walk with us on the road we choose to take. If we ask Him to, God can keep us from being who we are insisting on being—especially when it goes against our purpose in life.

The hardening of Pharaoh's heart is a part of God's judgment for the king's evil and oppressive ways. Pharaoh's insistence on being who he is sets the stage for God to judge both Pharaoh and Egypt and to display His power on behalf of His people.

"... Then I will lay my hand on Egypt and with mighty acts of judgment I will bring out my divisions, my people the Israelites. And the Egyptians will know that I am the Lord when I stretch out my hand against Egypt and bring the Israelites out of it." (Exodus 7:4–5)

God hardens Pharaoh's heart to make Moses' job harder so that, on the other side of victory, everyone would know that it is God who does the saving.

In Exodus 5:2, Pharaoh says, "Who is the Lord, that I should obey him and let Israel go? I do not know the Lord..." God is going to make sure that Pharaoh knows who God is.

What is God's word for you in your season? Is He asking you to keep being who you are being, or is He asking you to change your heart?

KEY POINTS

- As you embark on your journey of purpose, always keep your heart and mind open to hearing the Word of God for correction, redirection, and reaffirmation of your calling.

- Do not be surprised when you face opposition on your journey. Overcoming adversity is often God's way of displaying His power and provision.

- No matter what you encounter on your journey, keep your focus on God. Despite any circumstances to the contrary, God will maintain His purpose in keeping you and your calling on track.

REFLECT ON THE SCRIPTURE

"And the Egyptians will know that I am the Lord when I stretch out my hand against Egypt and bring the Israelites out of it." (Exodus 7:5)

1. What would it be like if God dealt with us at the level of standards—our, other people's, or the world's standards—instead of dealing with us at the level of our struggles?

2. Why would God tell the Israelites (and us) the "whole story" that includes painful experiences and the cost of following God?

3. Why would God allow Pharaoh to be who he insists on being, even if it goes against God's purpose? Why would God allow us to do so?

REFLECT ON YOUR JOURNEY

1. How did God "find" you? What are the differences between the person you were when God *found* you and the person God is *making* you to be now?

2. When have you had seasons of self-doubt?

3. When has God affirmed or reaffirmed your purpose?

4. What choices can bring you closer to who God is making you to be or take you on a detour away from God's purpose for you?

5. What is God's word for you in your season right now?

PRAYER FOR THE JOURNEY

Our God and our Father, we thank You for being a lamp unto our feet and a light unto our path. Even as we launch our journey to purpose, help us to continue listening to Your Word so that our will may always align with Yours. When we encounter circumstances that may oppose us and discourage us, give us the strength and wisdom to remain faithful in our journey, knowing that Your grace and power will lead us to victory. Mold us and shape us so that we will not only accomplish Your purpose but will also do it in a way that conforms to who and what You want us to be. We pray these blessings in Jesus' name and for His sake. Amen.

CHAPTER 6

Heart Trouble

The story of Moses and the Israelites teaches us that the journey to purpose and the actualization of dreams is usually paved with problems and difficulties. The bulk of the Exodus story is spent describing what Moses and the people have to overcome. No matter how noble your cause, how resolute your conviction, or how clear your calling from God, you will still have to deal with the obstacles between you and fulfillment. Sometimes circumstances block you and sometimes people do. Moses does not jump from a burning bush experience to the Promised Land; Pharaoh is in between. It's how we deal with obstacles that determines whether or not we make it to where we are intended to be!

Can you hold true to your path even when you encounter opposition? Can you keep moving forward even when the fire of momentum has almost been extinguished?

Read about the miraculous obstacles in Exodus Chapters 7–9.

YOU WILL HAVE TO OVERCOME MANY OBSTACLES ON YOUR JOURNEY.

Pharaoh is the main obstacle between Moses, the Israelites, and their journey to purpose. When Moses and Aaron go before Pharaoh and say, "Let my people go," Pharaoh says, "No!"

Injustice does not relent just because you tell it to. Change is not inevitable. The oppressor does not willingly give up oppression. The king's hand has to be forced. Martin Luther King, Jr. makes this clear in "Letter from Birmingham Jail":

"Injustice anywhere is a threat to justice everywhere. We are caught in an inescapable network of mutuality, tied in a single garment of destiny. Whatever affects one directly, affects all indirectly...

We know through painful experience that freedom is never voluntarily given by the oppressor; it must be demanded by the oppressed. Frankly, I have yet to engage in a direct action campaign that was 'well timed' in the view of those who have not suffered unduly from the disease of segregation. For years now I have heard the word 'Wait!' ... This 'Wait' has almost always meant 'Never.' We must come to see, with one of our distinguished jurists, that 'justice too long delayed is justice denied.'"

King's critics contended that if King just gave history time to unfold, injustice would go away and its victims would be freed. But King passionately responded that perpetrators of hatred and discrimination do not voluntarily give up their oppression. Direct action is needed. Hunger does not voluntarily release its chokehold. Profiling does not suddenly open its eyes to equality. Domestic violence does not simply dissolve into domestic bliss. Evil must be confronted.

Pharaoh refused to let the people go because of his "hard heart." His heart trouble was not coronary artery disease or congestive heart failure. It had nothing to do with arrhythmia, in which the heart beats with an irregular or abnormal rhythm. The Exodus narrative tells us that Pharaoh's heart is hard: *"Yet Pharaoh's heart became hard and he would not listen to them" (Exodus 7:13).*

Both Hebrew and Greek philosophy hold that the heart is the seat of emotions, will, and sensitivity. A hard heart is beyond the influence of external forces. Nothing can get to it! Sometimes, a heart that has been broken so many times can refuse to give itself to anyone else. In some cases, a hard heart is apathetic—showing and feeling no emotions. It is insensitive to the hurts and needs of those around it. A hard heart can't be touched by suffering or impacted by poverty. In a word, our society has "hard heart" disease.

Worst of all, a hard heart can be impervious to the nudging and promptings of God. It is a heart which has lost its sensitivity to the spiritual.

Jesus tells the parable of the seed and the sower:

"A farmer went out to sow his seed. As he was scattering the seed, some fell along the path; it was trampled on, and the birds ate it up. Some fell on rocky ground, and when it came up, the plants withered because they had no moisture. Other seed fell among thorns, which grew up with it and choked the plants. Still other seed fell on good soil. It came up and yielded a crop, a hundred times more than was sown." (Luke 8:5–8)

The seed that fell on the path was ground that people constantly walked on and, consequently, it had become so hard that it couldn't be penetrated. The seed simply bounced off the callous surface and the birds swooped down and immediately devoured it.

Jesus then explains the parable:

"This is the meaning of the parable: The seed is the word of God. Those along the path are the

ones who hear, and then the devil comes and takes away the word from their hearts, so that they may not believe and be saved. Those on the rocky ground are the ones who receive the word with joy when they hear it, but they have no root. They believe for a while, but in the time of testing they fall away. The seed that fell among thorns stands for those who hear, but as they go on their way they are choked by life's worries, riches and pleasures, and they do not mature. But the seed on good soil stands for those with a noble and good heart, who hear the word, retain it, and by persevering produce a crop." (Luke 8:11–15)

A hard heart can drift so far away from God that the things of God no longer matter like they used to. Sin, disappointment, and monotony can harden your heart. Your heart can be hardened by the experience of being let down by someone you trusted. Overexposure to things—even spiritual ones—can harden your heart toward them. If we hear the Word of God being faithfully explained and we fall asleep or ignore it, that could be a symptom of heart trouble.

Pharaoh is having this kind of heart trouble. His hard heart is exposed by how he responds to the plagues in this section of Exodus. God is trying to tell Pharaoh something, but it's clear that Pharaoh's heart has lost its sensitivity. Look at how many times Pharaoh's heart is hardened:

Pharaoh hardening his own heart	God hardening Pharaoh's heart
Exodus 7:13, 22	Exodus 9:12
Exodus 8:15, 19, 32	Exodus 10:27
Exodus 9:25-34	Exodus 11:10
Exodus 10:20, 27	

When God hardens Pharaoh's heart, God is allowing his heart to stay in the land of unrelenting stubbornness that Pharaoh has originally chosen to inhabit. Notice that God helps to harden Pharaoh's heart only after Pharaoh himself has hardened it five times over.

A HARD HEART CAN MAKE YOU HARD OF HEARING.

When Moses goes to Pharaoh with the same refrain, "let my people go," Pharaoh can't say that he doesn't understand it—he simply wants Moses to say something else. But Moses' message from God *can't* change until Pharaoh gets the original message.

God will first send us His word. The hope is that we understand and act upon it when we hear it.

Because the message isn't being received, Moses warns Pharaoh about the consequences:

"If you refuse to let them go, I will send a plague of frogs on your whole country." (Exodus 8:2)

"If you do not let my people go, I will send swarms of flies on you and your officials, on your people and into your houses." (Exodus 8:21)

If you refuse to let them go and continue to hold them back, the hand of the Lord will bring a terrible plague on your livestock in the field— on your horses, donkeys and camels and on your cattle, sheep and goats. (Exodus 9:2-3)

..."Let my people go, so that they may worship me, or this time I will send the full force of my plagues against you and against your officials and your people, so you may know that there is no one like me in all the earth.' (Exodus 9:13-14)

God warns Pharaoh multiple times because God wants to avoid sending the plagues if He doesn't have to. If God really wanted to punish Pharaoh and Egypt, God could have sent the plagues without a warning. God is patient, so for as long as possible God comes to us with His word.

'For by now I could have stretched out my hand and struck you and your people with a plague that would have wiped you off the earth.' (Exodus 9:15)

By now, the hand of God could have destroyed Pharaoh and the Egyptian people. Do we know what could have been the case for us "by now"? Some of us are unaware of what our condition could have been, had it not been for God's grace. Many of us could be deliberately choosing to turn our backs on our purpose and run in the opposite direction. Are you one of these "by now" people? Pharaoh certainly is, so Moses has to tell him God's word of the next plague:

> *'You still set yourself against my people and will not let them go. Therefore, at this time tomorrow I will send the worst hailstorm that has ever fallen on Egypt, from the day it was founded till now.' (Exodus 9:17–18)*

At this point, some Egyptian officials hear God's word and listen; they take their livestock and slaves inside. But Pharaoh and others do not heed God's word. They can't. Their hearts are so hard that the word of God has no effect.

If your heart ever gets so hard that you can't hear God's word, ask God to soften your heart. Even if the word is challenging or hits some vulnerable places, never just ignore it. God can melt your heart and reshape it to serve your purpose!

SOMETIMES, GOD SPEAKS TO US THROUGH THE MEDIUM OF MISERY.

Moses declares that if Pharaoh does not let the people go, God will send a hailstorm. That word is ignored, and the Lord tells Moses to stretch out his hand toward the sky. When Moses stretches his hand to the sky, the heavens open up and the storm is released. The hail was so large that it damaged everything. It was the worst storm in Egypt's history. Structures were damaged. Both people and livestock lost their lives.

All of the plagues represent nature being out of control. In this plague, along with the others, chaos is unleashed. Pharaoh's disobedience leads to chaos. The cosmic system reverts back to a pre-creation existence. Order is disturbed. The cosmos is interrupted. Pharaoh's actions on an ethical level lead to cosmic consequences.

When Moses stretched out his staff toward the sky, the Lord sent thunder and hail, and lightning flashed down to the ground. So the Lord rained hail on the land of Egypt; hail fell and lightning flashed back and forth. It was the worst storm in all the land of Egypt since it had become a nation. Throughout Egypt hail struck everything in the fields—both people and animals; it beat down everything growing in the fields and stripped every tree. (Exodus 8:23-25)

Pharaoh's heart is insensitive to the misery both he and his people experience. Pharaoh does not listen to the Word, but God has other ways of speaking. God can speak through a storm. Not all storms are of the devil. Some storms are caused or allowed by God. God would rather get our attention through less traumatic methods and circumstances, but if we don't seem to understand, God can speak in a language that increases the probability of our response.

The hailstorm is God's attempt to speak Pharaoh's language. God knows how to speak whatever language you speak. God is not just bilingual; God is multi-lingual. For some of us, it takes a storm to wake us up. God is so anxious for us to hear Him that He speaks in ways we are sure to hear Him. As strange as it might seem, we may want to thank God for these storms.

The glimmer of blessing for the Israelites is that this hailstorm hits everywhere in Egypt except one place:

The only place it did not hail was the land of Goshen, where the Israelites were. (Exodus 8:26)

In the midst of this stormy season created by Pharaoh's stubbornness, God's people are spared. One way or another, God has a way of protecting God's people—and God has a way of covering us in the storm.

GOD'S GRACE AND MERCY ARE NOT GIVEN TO SIMPLY GIVE US ANOTHER CHANCE. THEY ARE MEANT TO TRANSFORM US.

The same God who speaks to us through a message, and sometimes misery, will also speak to us through grace and mercy. During a conference on comparative religions, world-renowned experts were debating what (if any) belief was unique to Christianity. The debate went on for some time until C.S. Lewis, a writer and theologian, came into the room. He said, "Oh, that's easy. It's grace."

Grace is God's love for us given freely and without condition. We don't have to love God for Him to love us. God loves us whether we know Him or not, whether we listen to Him or not. That's grace. Grace is not a license to sin. It is a motivation to love.

The irony for Pharaoh and Egypt is that while God's judgment is in the hailstorm, He is also raining down grace and mercy. God doesn't allow everything to be destroyed in the storm.

(The flax and barley were destroyed, since the barley had headed and the flax was in bloom. The wheat and spelt, however, were not destroyed, because they ripen later.) (Exodus 9:31–32)

Even after the storm, there is something leftover. The wheat crops could restore Egypt's prosperity. In that time, barley was a less expensive grain than wheat. What is saved from the storm is worth more than what was lost. That's grace and mercy!

In the storms along your journey, you may have lost things. But while you're crying over the barley, don't forget to rejoice over the wheat!

Grace and mercy have the potential to change us. After going through the storms of plagues, Pharaoh finally has a change of heart.

Then Pharaoh summoned Moses and Aaron. "This time I have sinned," he said to them. "The Lord is in the right, and I and my people are in the wrong. Pray to the Lord, for we have had enough thunder and hail. I will let you go; you don't have to stay any longer." (Exodus 9:27-28)

Moses intercedes on behalf of Pharaoh and Egypt—and God stops the storm!

In some cases, God is just waiting for someone to pray. Is there a storm that God is using to speak to you right now? If so, pray!

KEY POINTS

- Nobody ever said the journey would be easy; obstacles and roadblocks should be anticipated.

- Our heart is at the very core of our understanding of our relationship to God.

- If we harden our hearts toward God, He may allow us to drift even further away from Him.

- Even though we may suffer from a hardened heart, God can forestall His judgment of us and, through His grace, offer us the benefit of another chance.

- Only God can transform a heart of stone into a heart of soul.

REFLECT ON THE SCRIPTURE

So Pharaoh's heart was hard and he would not let the Israelites go, just as the Lord had said through Moses. (Exodus 9:35)

1. Recall that Pharaoh hardens his own heart five times before God helps harden it. Why do you think Pharaoh would choose to be so hard-hearted?

2. As the leader of a nation, how are Pharaoh's attitude and behavior affecting the people he leads?

3. Moses has to repeat God's message again and again to Pharaoh. Why does he persevere?

4. If our society has "hard heart" disease, what is the cure?

REFLECT ON YOUR JOURNEY

1. What obstacles to your purpose are you currently experiencing?

2. When have you had the same message from God spoken into your life, perhaps multiple times? Did you listen to the message? Why or why not?

3. Where on your journey have you had a hard heart?

4. What are some steps that you took, or can take, toward softening your heart to God's desired direction for your life?

5. What storms have you encountered along your journey? What did you have to rejoice over when the storms were over?

6. What would be your prayer to God at this point in your journey?

PRAYER FOR THE JOURNEY

God of Abraham, Isaac, and Jacob, we acknowledge You as the rightful authority in our lives. We confess that we do not always give You the honor that You so rightly deserve. Even as we attempt to be obedient in allowing You to order our steps, we often rely upon ourselves to chart a path of our own design in this journey to purpose. We ask You now to soften and open our hearts to Your Word and Your promptings. As we listen, let our hearts both hear and respond to Your guidance as You offer us another chance. We thank You for Your mercy and Your grace. Help guide our thoughts, attitudes, and actions so that we can stay on Your path. We pray this in Christ's name. Amen.

CHAPTER 7

KEEP IT ALIVE

Even when we settle for less, God does not! Even when we choose to live beneath our purpose, God demands more. Even when we adjust our standards, God doesn't adjust His. God refuses to give up on us, even when we give up on ourselves. God believes in our dreams even when we have mothballed them and stored them away in the attic of no hope.

When we have been in a condition for a long time, we have a tendency to settle for it. No matter how much they had settled for Egypt, the Israelites were not meant for bondage; they were meant for the freedom of the Promised Land. However, to get out of Egypt, they first had to deal with an obstacle called Pharaoh who stood in the way between where they were and where they were meant to be. Moses came with one message for Pharaoh, "Let my people go," but Pharaoh did not listen. In fact, Pharaoh challenged God by questioning both His existence and significance. Therefore, a part of God's motivation was not only to free the people but to show Pharaoh who He was. So, the plagues were unleashed on Egypt. The brief but intense pain and suffering would cause Pharaoh to relent, but his decision to let the people go lasted only as long as the pain of plague lasted. As soon as that wore off, he went back to business as usual.

Pharaoh's response was not one of repentance; it was remorse for having to deal with the consequences of his hard heart. Remorse is a response of your emotion; repentance is a response of your will. The response of your emotion lasts as long as the pain of the consequences lasts. As soon as the memory of the consequences fades so does the decision to do right.

Read Exodus Chapters 10–12.

THERE IS A RELATIONSHIP BETWEEN THE SHEDDING OF BLOOD AND THE FULFILLMENT OF PURPOSE.

In the last plague, there would be a night in which the death angel would visit Egyptian families, their first born, and their animals. In order for the death angel to "pass over" the homes of the Israelites and spare their firstborn, they would have to slaughter a lamb, smear the blood on the doorposts and the beam above the doorway, and stay inside the house. This "covering by the blood" would lead to the deliverance of the people from Egypt.

God gives Moses instructions as to how the Passover is to take place, including slaying the lamb and preparing the meal, which should be eaten on the eve of the people's deliverance. God also tells Moses to ritualize the actions of that night.

"Obey these instructions as a lasting ordinance for you and your descendants. When you enter the land that the Lord will give you as he promised, observe this ceremony. And when your children ask you, 'What does this ceremony mean to you?' then tell them, 'It is the Passover sacrifice to the Lord, who passed over the houses of the Israelites in Egypt and spared our homes when he struck down the Egyptians.'" Then the people bowed down and worshiped. The Israelites did just what the Lord commanded Moses and Aaron. (Exodus 12:24–28)

The activity of that night of Passover was to become a perpetual, annual ritual.

RITUALS ENABLE US TO PARTICIPATE IN THE REALITY OF THE EXPERIENCE LONG AFTER THE EXPERIENCE IS OVER.

The intention of this ceremony is to keep the event alive. God does not want the reality of the event to die. Even though pain and memories of bondage are associated with this act of deliverance, God wants the Israelites to keep this experience alive. God knows that once they reach the Promised Land, the Israelites may forget about what happened. It's tempting to forget the hardships of the journey once you have arrived— to forget about the people who have sacrificed for you. Arriving tends to give us amnesia. God does not want the Israelites to forget about their deliverance—or us to forget about ours.

The last thing we want to do is to forget about our deliverance. Sometimes, we are "saved" for so long that we forget about how we got saved. We forget about how God has given us new life. We get complacent about worshipping God and thanking Him for His act of deliverance. When we forget, we become ungrateful and complaining becomes a way of life.

In order to keep the experience alive, the Lord wants the Israelites to observe and even "guard" the ceremony. Years after the deliverance, they were to slaughter the Passover lambs, and consume some of the lamb. They were to eat bitter herbs. They were to drink the wine. They were to eat bread without yeast. Each time they did that, they would remember the experience of their deliverance. Keep it alive! Keep it alive by observing the ritual.

RITUALS KEEP EXPERIENCES ALIVE.

The act of Communion is not undertaken merely out of habit; Jesus gives us the ritual to keep our salvation at the cross alive.

And he took bread, gave thanks and broke it, and gave it to them, saying, "This is my body given for you; do this in remembrance of me." In the same way, after the supper he took the cup, saying, "This cup is the new covenant in my blood, which is poured out for you. (Luke 22:19-20)

The bread is broken because Jesus' body was broken. The cup of wine or juice is shared because Jesus shed His blood. The deliverance that came on the cross can't be forgotten. The fact that Jesus shed His blood can't die. The fact that He is risen can't die!

GOD SEES FOR US WHAT WE CAN'T SEE FOR OURSELVES.

The people are given a ritual even before they experience the reality. At the moment, they are still slaves in Egypt, but they are given a ritual which anticipates liberation and freedom.

"This is a day you are to commemorate; for the generations to come you shall celebrate it

as a festival to the Lord—a lasting ordinance."
(Exodus 12:14)

God is so confident about victory that He plans the celebration *before* the Israelites get to the Promised Land. God already sees them beyond where they are—living in their intended purpose. Even if they can't see it, God can see it for them.

When the Lord has promised you something, you can start dancing and shouting long before you see the finish line. Even if you are in the same condition that you've been in, you can initiate your celebration. Perhaps you are still in Egypt, wrestling with some of the same issues the Israelites wrestled with. You can perfect your ritual while you are still in Egypt and practice your praise for when you come out!

OBSERVING CEREMONY CREATES AN INTEREST.

Moses is telling the Israelites to keep the experience alive by observing the ceremony of Passover.

And when your children ask you, 'What does this ceremony mean to you?' then tell them, 'It is the Passover sacrifice to the Lord, who passed over the houses of the Israelites in Egypt and spared our homes when he struck down the Egyptians.'"
(Exodus 12:26-27)

By observing the ceremony, they would create an interest for their children who would know nothing about Pharaoh and bondage, making bricks without straw, or spreading blood on doorposts.

The only way the young people would know what happened is if they asked questions about what they had observed. It would be strange for them to see lambs being slaughtered and their parents dressing a certain way for this ceremony. Observation would seize their attention and pique their interest in the faith. Children can be told something over and over again without the words ever sinking in. But when they *see* a ceremony or an event for themselves, then they are engaged. What gets their attention is not what they hear, but what they observe.

Perhaps our young people are not raising any questions about our faith because they aren't observing the right things. Is the world not raising any questions because our behavior is not piquing interest? Jesus looked at his disciples and said, *"By this everyone will know that you are my disciples, if you love one another" (John 13:35).*

When the world sees us taking care of each other, it raises some questions. When the world hears us defending each other instead of participating in tearing each other down, it will raise some questions. When people see us being serious about our worship, they will have questions. What would happen if our young people saw us making praise and worship a priority?

OUR FAITHFULNESS CAN STIR CURIOSITY.

The story of blind Bartimaeus is a great example of interest being piqued by someone making noise. As a crowd of people paraded through the streets of Jericho, a blind man on the side of the road noticed the commotion.

Then they came to Jericho. As Jesus and his disciples, together with a large crowd, were leaving the city, a blind man, Bartimaeus (which means "son of Timaeus"), was sitting by the roadside begging. When he heard that it was Jesus of Nazareth, he began to shout, "Jesus, Son of David, have mercy on me!"

Many rebuked him and told him to be quiet, but he shouted all the more, "Son of David, have mercy on me!"

Jesus stopped and said, "Call him."

So they called to the blind man, "Cheer up! On your feet! He's calling you." Throwing his cloak aside, he jumped to his feet and came to Jesus.

"What do you want me to do for you?" Jesus asked him.

The blind man said, "Rabbi, I want to see."

"Go," said Jesus, "your faith has healed you." Immediately he received his sight and followed Jesus along the road. (Mark 10:46–52)

If there had been no noise, Bartimaeus would have never asked the question. Had he never asked the question, he may never have pursued Jesus or been healed and delivered.

Likewise, our praise and worship can draw people's attention. During a hot summer night in St. Paul, Minnesota, the church was packed, and the windows were wide open. Both praise singing and the Holy Spirit resonated in the air. A man entered the open door and walked down the aisle. He shared that he had just been walking by when the sounds of praise made him curious. He stood outside the window listening to the story of Jesus who shed His blood for our sins. Questions kept coming up: Can you believe that God loves you enough that He sent His only Son to save you? Did you know that Jesus died for *you*? Did you know that, by believing in Jesus and His sacrifice, you can have the promise of an eternal life with God? That night, the man gave his life to Christ. Something ought to be happening in our ceremonies that raises questions!

WE HAVE A STORY TO TELL.

The Passover celebration was meant to grab the interest of the children so they would ask, "What does the ritual mean?" The raising of that question opens the door for testimony. The Israelites had a story that was too good to keep to themselves. It needed to be shared. They had a story because they had been through something.

You too have been journeying and, therefore, have a story. The way to keep a story alive is by continuing to talk about it. If you want certain stories to end, just stop talking about them. If you want negativity to die, stop talking about it. The children had a story and, by telling it, they would keep it alive.

What is the story? The story is that a lamb was slain. The slain lambs that the children of the Israelites see are symbolic of the Passover lambs that are slain the night that the Israelites are spared. The wrath of God hits the households in Egypt, but the households of the Israelites are spared because they are covered by the blood of the lambs, the sign that God will spare them. Not only were the Israelites spared, but their enemies were dealt with. Is this your story, too?

All of this happened to the Israelites because of the blood of a lamb. We have a story too, but it's not because of many lambs, it's because of One Lamb. Jesus' blood is at the heart of our stories. According to Jesus' betrayer, Judas, it's innocent blood.

When Judas, who had betrayed him, saw that Jesus was condemned, he was seized with remorse and returned the thirty pieces of silver to the chief priests and the elders. "I have sinned," he said, "for I have betrayed innocent blood."(Matthew 27:3-4)

According to a faithful disciple, Peter, it's precious blood.

"For you know that it was not with perishable things such as silver or gold that you were redeemed from the empty way of life handed down to you from your ancestors, but with the precious blood of Christ, a lamb without blemish or defect. He was chosen before the creation of the world, but was revealed in these last times for your sake. Through him you believe in God, who raised him from the dead and glorified him, and so your faith and hope are in God." (1 Peter 1: 18–21)

According to another disciple, John, it's cleansing blood.

"But if we walk in the light, as he is in the light, we have fellowship with one another, and the blood of Jesus, his Son, cleanses us from all sin." (1 John 1:7, English Standard Version)

According to yet another testifying disciple, Paul, it's purchasing, justifying, and peacemaking blood.

"Keep watch over yourselves and all the flock of which the Holy Spirit has made you overseers. Be shepherds of the church of God, which he bought with his own blood." (Acts 20:28)

"Since we have now been justified by his blood, how much more shall we be saved from God's wrath through him!" (Romans 5:9)

"The Son is the image of the invisible God, the firstborn over all creation. ... For God was pleased to have all his fullness dwell in him, and through him to reconcile to himself all things, whether things on earth or things in heaven, by making peace through his blood, shed on the cross." (Colossians 1:15, 19–20)

The Israelites were able to make it through the dangers of Egypt because they were covered by the blood. Today, we are covered by the blood of Jesus. You can make it through enemy territory because you are covered by His blood!

Keep that alive. Tell somebody about that!

KEY POINTS

In God's economy, the shedding of blood is a spiritual act that symbolically represents the washing away of sins—the foundation of our salvation.

Two ceremonial rituals initiated by God involve the shedding of blood:

1. In the Old Testament, the story of the blood of lambs delivers the Hebrew people from captivity.

2. In the New Testament, the story of the blood of the Lamb of God delivers humankind from the bondage of sin.

God's use of rituals serves two purposes:

1. To keep alive what He has done and what He has promised to us.

2. To communicate our story in a way that will generate interest in others.

REFLECT ON THE SCRIPTURE

"Obey these instructions as a lasting ordinance for you and your descendants." (Exodus 12:24)

1. How would you describe the relationship between the shedding of blood and the fulfillment of purpose?

2. How do ceremonies, like Passover, testify about our faith?

3. None of us experienced the plagues and God's deliverance or witnessed Jesus' sacrifice firsthand. As children of past observers, what is our responsibility for the present and future generations?

4. How do rituals, like Communion, keep experiences alive?

REFLECT ON YOUR JOURNEY

1. What do you think God might be seeing for you that you can't see for yourself?

2. How can you practice your praise for when you come out "on the other side"?

3. What ceremonies/rituals have shaped your experience of God, Jesus, and the Holy Spirit?

4. What questions have been raised for you?

5. At this point in your journey, what is your story?

6. How can you keep your story alive? Name at least three ways that you can share your story—and share it!

PRAYER FOR THE JOURNEY

Dear Lord, author and finisher of our faith, we lift our voices in praise for delivering us from the bondage of sin. We thank you for Your mercy and grace in redeeming us. We are grateful for the rituals that help us remember what You have done for us. We are amazed that You gave Your precious Son as a ransom for our disobediences. His shed blood saved us from the penalty of sin, the practice of sin, and, ultimately, the very presence of sin. Help us to not just rest in the contentment we might have of our salvation, but keep us mindful that Your rituals, Your worship, and Your praise call us to remember the awesome nature of Your power and goodness. May we remain steadfast and humble in our faithfulness to You so that our story may draw others into Your Kingdom. We pray this in the marvelous and magnificent name of our Savior, Jesus Christ. Amen.

CHAPTER 8

LEARNING TO LEAN

The Exodus story is really a story about faith. When God first calls Moses to deliver the Israelites from bondage, Moses struggles with trust. He asks God a series of questions:

"Who am I that I should go to Pharaoh and bring the Israelites out of Egypt?" (Exodus 3:11)

"Suppose I go to the Israelites and say to them, 'The God of your fathers has sent me to you,' and they ask me, 'What is his name?' Then what shall I tell them?'" (Exodus 3:13)

Moses answered, "What if they do not believe me or listen to me and say, 'The Lord did not appear to you'?" (Exodus 4:1)

The questions even turn into an outright rejection of God's call:

But Moses said, "Pardon your servant, Lord. Please send someone else." (Exodus 4:13)

Then, once Moses goes to Pharaoh and the Israelites, faith remains at the center of the battle.

God tries to move the people into their purpose. They are not meant for bondage; they are meant for liberation and freedom. As God moves them, they struggle to believe Moses' message. They struggle with faith.

Have you ever wondered what makes purified water so pure? Purified water does not start pure; it takes a process to make it pure. Water is mechanically filtered or processed to remove the impurities and make it suitable for use. Distillation is one way to purify water. Water is boiled and the vapor is condensed into a container, leaving the contaminants behind. The main ingredient in this process is heat. When the heat is turned on, the impurities in the water are separated from the water. It takes heat to make the water suitable for use—just like it takes "the fire of the trials of faith" to make us suitable for God's use.

Read Exodus Chapters 13–15.

FAITH IS RARELY PURE.

Contaminants of doubt live in faith. There are very few instances when our faith does not have elements of doubt. We like to make people think our faith is pure. We don't want anyone to get a glimpse of our stubborn doubt. Many of us waver between faith and doubt. We want to believe; we want to trust God; we want to lean on God's word, but there are seasons when it is difficult. We trust God one moment, and we panic the next. When we see the word of God come alive during the day, we are ready to lean on God, but then that night we vacillate in our faith and wonder how everything is going to work out.

As the saga continues, God displays His strength by unleashing a series of plagues. Eventually, Pharaoh relents enough for the Israelites to escape. Once they escape, God leads them with a cloud by day and fire by night.

By day the Lord went ahead of them in a pillar of cloud to guide them on their way and by night in a pillar of fire to give them light, so that they could travel by day or night. (Exodus 13:21)

The same God who gets you out of what you're in will lead you to where He wants you to be.

As God leads them, the people of God still wrestle with believing in this God. After Pharaoh lets the Israelites go, he realizes that he just lost free labor and decides to go after them. He gathers his soldiers and their chariots, and they pursue the Israelites. When God's people see Pharaoh and his army behind them, they express their lack of trust.

They said to Moses, "Was it because there were no graves in Egypt that you brought us to the desert to die? What have you done to us by bringing us out of Egypt? Didn't we say to you in Egypt, 'Leave us alone; let us serve the Egyptians'? It would have been better for us to serve the Egyptians than to die in the desert!" (Exodus 14:11-12)

They tell Moses that serving the Egyptians in bondage is better than being on the journey toward freedom! This is much more than a statement of frustration with Moses; it is a statement of a lack of trust in God.

SOMETIMES YOU HAVE TO TRUST YOUR WAY INTO TRUST.

Even as the Israelites walk with God, they have issues trusting God—and we should applaud them because at least they *keep* walking with God. This is a good reminder for us today. Even when you wonder about God and whether or not God will make a way, keep walking with God. Even when you are having a crisis of faith, keep worshipping God. Even if you think the prayers are not being heard—keep praying. Stay on the road with God. An imperfect faith still has to stay on the journey toward purpose.

The reason you want to walk with God even when you don't totally trust God is because there will be times along the way that God will purify your faith. When the heat is turned up, and God must show Himself strong, the impurities of doubt will dissipate into thin air. The redemptive activity of God is one way that God teaches us to lean on Him. Some of us are on the other side of the purification. Your faith is purified not because of what you read in a book or because you attended a faith conference. Your faith goes through development and purification because of some hot seasons. It takes some heat to make us suitable for use. As James, one of Jesus' disciples, says:

Consider it pure joy, my brothers and sisters, whenever you face trials of many kinds, because you know that the testing of your faith produces perseverance. (James 1:2–3)

The Israelites endure experiences that teach them how to lean on God. The more they lean on God, the more they learn how to lean.

CHANGE STARTS BECAUSE OF THE ACTIVITY OF GOD.

This change in the Israelites starts because of the activity of God. They have left Pharaoh. But Pharaoh is behind them. They can't escape to the right or left because of the mountains, and they can't go forward because of the Red Sea. They could not go around the sea; they had to go through it.

Then Moses stretched out his hand over the sea, and all that night the Lord drove the sea back with a strong east wind and turned it into dry land. The waters were divided, and the Israelites went through the season dry ground, with a wall of water on their right and on their left. (Exodus 14:21–22)

There are some things you can't go around—you must go through. As you go through, however, God will step ahead of you and part what you can't part yourself.

As you move forward on the path God has put you on, there will be obstacles that you can't move yourself. Those are the obstacles that God can move—and many times He will move them. The Israelites have to continue to walk as though they are going through. When they take the steps to go through their obstacle, God opens up the way. Has God ever provided a way for *you*?

Some ways will not open up until we decide to go through. Sometimes we may not experience the hand of God moving in our situations because we want to go around. As we decide to go through, a way is made. God makes a way so well that the Israelites go through on dry ground. They don't even have to walk in mud! God dries up the floor of the sea!

Not only is a way made, but a wall is formed. The narrator tells us that the water forms walls on both sides. The water that had been an obstacle now becomes an ally for the Israelites. The same water that was keeping them from their destiny is now helping them to get there. The same water that caused fear is now serving the cause. Along the way of purpose, God can recalibrate and reorder your obstacles. The very people and situation that blocks you, ends up assisting you.

The Egyptians see how the Israelites make it through the sea. They become overconfident and think that they can make it through what God's people made it through. The pursuing Egyptians attempt to go through the same sea that the Israelites go through, but the same water that saves the Israelites drowns the Egyptians. The Egyptians soon discover that the Israelites "making it through" has nothing to do with the Israelites—it has everything to do with God.

That day the Lord saved Israel from the hands of the Egyptians, and Israel saw the Egyptians lying dead on the shore. And when the Israelites saw the mighty hand of the Lord displayed against the Egyptians, the people feared the Lord and put their trust in him and in Moses his servant. (Exodus 14:30–31)

When God's hand is on you, you can make it through what others can't make it through. Some of us make it through Red Seas that we should not have. Other folks try to make it through that sea, and do not make it! Some of us pursue dreams and goals which we can never hope to accomplish without the mighty hand of God. Put your trust in God!

GOD EQUIPS YOU FOR WHAT IS COMING NEXT.

The Egyptians pursuing the Israelites are military soldiers with sophisticated weaponry—swords, spears, chariots, and horses—of which the Israelites have none.

The Egyptians pursued them, and all Pharaoh's horses and chariots and horsemen followed them into the sea. During the last watch of the night the Lord looked down from the pillar of fire and cloud at the Egyptian army and threw it into confusion. He jammed the wheels of their chariots so that they had difficulty driving. And the Egyptians said, "Let's get away from the Israelites! The Lord is fighting for them against Egypt."

Then the Lord said to Moses, "Stretch out your hand over the sea so that the waters may flow back over the Egyptians and their chariots and horsemen." Moses stretched out his hand over the sea, and at daybreak the sea went back to its place. The Egyptians were fleeing toward it, and the Lord swept them into the sea. The water flowed back and covered the chariots and horsemen—the entire army of Pharaoh that had followed the Israelites into the sea. Not one of them survived. (Exodus 14:23–28)

After the Egyptian warriors are defeated, all of their weapons become available to the Israelites.

But this is not going to be their last conflict. Later on, in the wilderness, the Israelites encounter other enemies, and they are able to fight with weapons they secured from the Egyptians. Victorious in battle, the Israelites acquire weaponry for future battles. From the battle they were in, they came out with weapons to use in future battles. God gives them weapons from a past battle to use in future battles.

God doesn't just bring you out of struggles empty-handed. He gives you something to help you deal with the next battle.

GOD'S ACTIVITY LEADS TO OUR AWARENESS.

The actions of the Egyptians demonstrate the futility of fighting against God. The Israelites witness God's great power over the Egyptians because the Egyptians are on their trail. The Egyptians pursue the Israelites because Pharaoh decides to come after them, and Pharaoh makes his decision because God hardens his heart after Pharaoh had decided to let them go.

The Lord hardened the heart of Pharaoh king of Egypt, so that he pursued the Israelites, who were marching out boldly. (Exodus 14:8)

Remember that Pharaoh's heart was hardened 11 times in Chapters 7–11 of Exodus (see Chapter 6 of this book). When God hardens Pharaoh's heart, God is allowing his heart to remain in the initial state that Pharaoh chooses to be in—unrelenting and stubborn.

Why would God do that? Why would God cause your enemies to come after you? Why would God choose to incite your foes?

We can be certain that, at this point, Moses is more than tired of dealing with Pharaoh. Just when he thinks he is rid of the enemy, he turns around and, like a recurring sickness, there is his nemesis! Why would God allow that?

Why does God allow your enemies to remain close? Exodus 14 gives us an answer.

God allows the Egyptians to stay on Moses' trail so that he can see what happens when God deals with them. The Israelites see the Egyptians wash up on the seashore. None of us should rejoice in the death of anyone, even these Egyptians. However, the death of the Egyptians is more than the death of some individuals who followed the orders of a hard-hearted leader; it is about the death of evil.

God wants the Israelites to see the death of evil. Evil does die. As entrenched as it is, one day the evil of terrorism will die. God keeps our enemies close so that we can see the death of evil.

NOT EVERYONE ATTRIBUTES GOD'S ACTIVITY TO GOD.

The parting of the waters of the Red Sea was an act of nature, but, having seen it, the Israelites attribute it to God. Followers of God see what other people don't see or refuse to see. Some people refuse to see the hand of God operating in life and history. And, some of them, because of spiritual blindness, are incapable of seeing the hand of God moving in their own lives. It takes a heart conditioned by the Holy Spirit to be able to see God moving in events and life.

There's a story of a woman who, every time she takes her groceries in the house, would praise

God from the car to the porch. Her neighbor, who happens to be an atheist, gets tired of hearing all this praise for God, so he decides to play a trick on her. He buys her some groceries and puts them on her porch. Then he waits on his porch to see her reaction. When the woman pulls up in her driveway, she sees the food and goes from her car to the porch, shouting, "Thank you, Jesus! Thank you, Jesus!" Her neighbor smugly runs over to her and says, "Gotcha! Jesus had nothing to do with those groceries. I bought them for you." She then says to him, "Jesus had everything to do with those groceries. Jesus got me this food; He just used you to deliver it!"

It takes a heart of faith to see the hand of God in life's events. What others see as coincidence you might see as the hand of God!

AWARENESS LEADS TO AN ADVANCEMENT OF FAITH—LEANING ON THE LORD.

When we experience the hand of God, our faith increases. The Israelites witness the great power of God when they see the Egyptians dead on the seashore (Exodus 14:31).

On their journey, the Israelites learn how to lean on God. They hadn't been born leaning on God, and neither were any of us. The wise king Solomon reminds us that we should not lean on ourselves:

Trust in the Lord with all your heart and lean not on your own understanding; in all your ways submit to him, and he will make your paths straight. (Proverbs 3:5-6)

Some of us ought to be leaning on the Lord more now than we were five years ago because of what we've seen. Some of you have seen God heal your body. Some of you have seen God heal a broken heart. Some of you have seen God put food on the table. What have you seen lately?

In some ways, God earns the trust of the Israelites through the opening of the sea and the death of evil. They have been purified by the heat of a battle that God fights and wins for them. And yet, they still have a long way to go on their journey of faith. Look at what happens next.

Then Moses led Israel from the Red Sea and they went into the Desert of Shur. For three days they traveled in the desert without finding water. When they came to Marah, they could not drink its water because it was bitter. (That is why the place is called Marah.) So the people grumbled against Moses, saying, "What are we to drink?"

*Then Moses cried out to the Lord, and
the Lord showed him a piece of wood. He threw it
into the water, and the water became fit to drink.
... (Exodus 15:22–25)*

God remains faithful to His people. He purifies
the water so that they can drink it.

God has proven Himself able to sustain you. Are
you ready to lean?

KEY POINTS

1.   Faith almost never comes to us as a fully
      mature and pure relationship to God; it
      grows from experiences that cultivate our
      trust and diminish our doubts.

2.   The strengthening of our faith is initiated by
      God Himself, and all He asks of us is to:

      - Be aware of when and how He is working
        in our lives.

      - Remain open to His guidance and
        direction.

3.   Faith is an essential element of our journey to
      purpose. Our progress in this arena requires
      us to trust God when we cannot deal with our
      dilemmas, to depend upon Him to anticipate
      and answer our apprehensions, and to lean
      upon Him to lead us in every aspect of our lives.

REFLECT ON THE SCRIPTURE

But the Israelites went through the sea on dry ground, with a wall of water on their right and on their left. That day the Lord saved Israel from the hands of the Egyptians, and Israel saw the Egyptians lying dead on the shore. And when the Israelites saw the mighty hand of the Lord displayed against the Egyptians, the people feared the Lord and put their trust in him and in Moses his servant. (Exodus 14:29-31)

1. What are some examples of obstacles becoming allies for the Israelites?

2. What are some examples of obstacles becoming allies for you?

3. Why does God allow enemies to remain close?

4. How do we know that God's activity is really from God?

5. Why is it important to lean on God?

REFLECT ON YOUR JOURNEY

1. What experiences or trials have shaped you to be suitable for God's use?

2. What enemies are ahead of (or behind) you on your journey?

3. What has God given you to help you deal with the next battle?

4. Where do you see the hand of God in your life's events leading you toward your purpose?

5. How is God providing a way forward for you?

6. What do you still need in order to lean on God and trust God fully?

PRAYER FOR THE JOURNEY

Dear God, we come before you with humble hearts and acknowledge that all that we are and all that we hope to be is a gift from You. Although we trust in You, we confess that our faith sometimes wavers when we do not fully understand our circumstances and when we face challenges that cause us to be conflicted and confused. Forgive us for our doubts and our inadequacies. Fortify our faith as we move forward in this journey to purpose. You have been our dwelling place in all generations, and we pray now, as we face the continuation of our journey, that You will give us hearts and minds to seek and depend upon You. These things we ask in Jesus' name and for His sake. Amen.

CHAPTER 9

A Time to Dance

In the Book of Exodus, God calls a man to be a leader and a liberator who does not deserve to be either. Moses commits a heinous act by murdering an Egyptian and ruins his reputation among his people, but God calls him anyway. God's purpose for Moses outweighs Moses' mistakes; God still chooses and uses him. Moses and the Israelites take note of this and many other events:

- After Moses confronts Pharaoh and Pharaoh makes the situation worse, God sustains the Israelites. In the same way, God can sustain you when bad becomes worse.

- Pharaoh's refusal to let the Israelites go unleashes the wrath of God in the form of plagues throughout Egypt, and Pharaoh finally lets them go. In the face of opposition, God can make it so that the enemy just gets sick of you.

- Pursued by Pharaoh and his army, the Israelites arrive at the Red Sea, but they cannot cross it. God doesn't just open the sea. God dries the sea floor so that once they make it to the other side, there is no evidence that they have been through what they have come through. When facing a seemingly insurmountable obstacle, God can make the same sea which is *in* your way to help *make* a way.

- The Egyptians attempt to cross the dry sea floor like the Israelites, but the waters converge upon them and they perish. When the hand of God is on you, the path of deliverance for you can be the path of destruction for the enemy.

Reread Exodus Chapters 14 and 15.

TAKE NOTE OF GOD'S MANIFESTATIONS OF GRACE.

Notice how Chapter 15 differs from Chapter 14. Chapter 14 is filled with the prose of action (the activity of God) while Chapter 15 sings with the poetry of praise (the adoration for God). Deliverance gives birth to doxology, a formal expression of praise! If God is faithful in the Chapter 14 of our lives with action, then we need to be faithful in the Chapter 15 of our lives with adoration.

God summons us to pull over and acknowledge God's blessings on the journey. Have you taken note lately of God's recent manifestations of grace?

SHIFT FROM REHEARSING PAST ACTIONS TO DECLARING FUTURE ANTICIPATION.

In Chapter 15, Moses and the Israelites sing about what God has just done and about what God will do. The first half of the song celebrates God's actions, His salvation and strength.

"I will sing to the Lord, for he is highly exalted. Both horse and driver he has hurled into the sea. "The Lord is my strength and my defense; he has become my salvation. He is my God, and I will praise him, my father's God, and I will exalt him. The Lord is a warrior; the Lord is his name. Pharaoh's chariots and his army he has hurled into the sea. The best of Pharaoh's officers are drowned in the Red Sea. The deep waters have covered them; they sank to the depths like a stone. Your right hand, Lord, was majestic in power. Your right hand, Lord, shattered the enemy. (Exodus 15:1-6)

The end of the song shifts to declaring future anticipation.

You will bring them in and plant them on the mountain of your inheritance— the place, Lord, you made for your dwelling, the sanctuary, Lord, your hands established. (Exodus 15:17)

Moses and the Israelites have a present confidence about the future because of God's past actions. They understand that the Egyptians are not the last enemy they will encounter, but they can face their future foes with a new level of audacity because they know what God has already done.

TAKE TIME TO SAY THANK YOU TO THE PEOPLE WHO GET YOU WHERE YOU ARE SUPPOSED TO BE.

After Moses and the Israelites sing the song (Exodus 15:1–18), take note of who leads the next round of praise.

Then Miriam the prophet, Aaron's sister, took a timbrel in her hand, and all the women followed her, with timbrels and dancing. (Exodus 15:20)

Miriam's identity is connected to her being the sister of Aaron; she has no independent identity. She is known by her connections to her brothers. Moses and Aaron are the lead actors in the Exodus drama. However, without Miriam, Moses probably wouldn't even exist. She is the one who watches over Moses in his basket in the crocodile-infested Nile River. She is the one who connects their mother with Pharaoh's daughter, so that Moses' mother could serve as Moses' caretaker. Miriam is instrumental in making sure Moses gets to where he is supposed to be.

The identity of the "Miriams" of the world gets subsumed in the prominence of Moses and Aaron, but the role of Miriam is indispensable. Many of you have some Miriams in your life who deserve great gratitude because they watched over you as you drifted in dangerous waters. They made sure you got to where you are supposed to be. Take time to say thank you to your Miriams.

Miriam is further identified as a prophet. In the Bible, female prophets have the same role as male prophets—both are spokespersons for God. God uses Miriam's gifts. If God chooses a woman to be a prophet, who are we to argue?

Miriam is a prophet who leads her people in worship. This is significant. She has an important position, *and* she is a worshipper.

When some people become leaders or prominent figures, they stop praising God. Praise seems to be beneath them. People with positions need to know that it's alright to lift your hands in praise and say "Amen!" It's alright for prophets to run and dance.

As a matter of fact, you might want to praise God even louder. If God's grace can use you in your position in spite of who you are, God deserves loud praise!

WORSHIP DEMANDS A CONSCIOUSNESS OF SURROUNDING BLESSINGS.

Miriam the prophet leads one of the first worship services recorded in scripture. Notice that the praise occurs right after the narrator in Chapter 14 summarizes what has just happened:

> *But the Israelites went through the sea on dry ground, with a wall of water on their right and on their left. That day the Lord saved Israel from the hands of the Egyptians, and Israel saw the Egyptians lying dead on the shore. And when the Israelites saw the mighty hand of the Lord displayed against the Egyptians, the people feared the Lord and put their trust in him and in Moses his servant. (Exodus 14:29–31)*

Miriam, Moses, and all of the Israelites engage in praise right after they cross the sea—while they are still covered with the mist of the sea and can taste the saltwater in their mouths. There is no hesitation. Before there is consumption of God's blessings, there is recognition of God's blessings. The same folks who cried out to God while they were in bondage are now praising God in their freedom. If we cried out to God on *that* side of our burden, we need to shout out a thank you on *this* side of our blessing. If we cried out to God on *that* side of cancer, we need to praise God on *this* side of healing.

Many people who cry out to the Lord on *that* side forget about praising God on *this* side. An example is when Jesus heals ten lepers.

Now on his way to Jerusalem, Jesus traveled along the border between Samaria and Galilee. As he was going into a village, ten men who had leprosy met him. They stood at a distance and called out in a loud voice, "Jesus, Master, have pity on us!"

When he saw them, he said, "Go, show yourselves to the priests." And as they went, they were cleansed.

One of them, when he saw he was healed, came back, praising God in a loud voice. He threw himself at Jesus' feet and thanked him—and he was a Samaritan.

Jesus asked, "Were not all ten cleansed? Where are the other nine? Has no one returned to give praise to God except this foreigner?" Then he said to him, "Rise and go; your faith has made you well." (Luke 17:11–19)

On *that* side of healing the ten lepers cried out to Jesus, but on *this* side of healing only one returns to say thank you! If you have ever been on *that* side of trouble and God brings you to *this* side, it might be time to worship and praise God.

147

Miriam recognizes that it is God's hand that saves the Israelites. It is not military prowess or the simple cooperation of nature in the form of a strong wind that opens up the sea. It is all God's doing— and they respond immediately in praise.

Praise ceases sometimes because we lose sight of the Red Sea through which God has brought us. Some of you have a Red Sea that has been pushed to the far side of your memory. Every now and then, you need to recall it from your psychological archives and return to your Red Sea. You can only thank God for helping you through your Red Sea if you are aware of what God has done for you. Keep it alive in your memory just as God keeps you alive on *this* side of blessing.

THANK GOD FOR A CURRENT BLESSING, EVEN IF OTHER MOUNTAINS ARE DOWN THE ROAD.

Miriam and the Israelites praise God after just coming through the Red Sea. However, they are still not in the Promised Land. They still have to journey through the wilderness ahead of them. God's promise to them is not simply that He would get them *out* of something; the other part of the promise is that He will get them *into* something—the Promised Land. In between the Red Sea and Promised Land, they stop to praise God for a current victory even though the battle is not yet won.

148

Even if you haven't graduated, thank God for passing a course on the way to the goal. Even if you have not won the battle over grief, thank God for being able to get out of bed this morning. Even if you are not totally out of debt, thank Him for being able to pay a particular bill.

Miriam and the Israelites praise God during that "in between" time. This is the time when you are not quite where you want to be. You still have some hills to climb, and you don't know how life is going to turn out. Between jobs or relationships, praise God. During a pit stop on your journey to purpose, praise God.

WORSHIP STARTS IN THE HEART, BUT IT INCLUDES FULL-BODY EXPRESSION.

Notice how intense the Israelites' worship is. Miriam leads praise that involves playing an instrument, singing a song, and dancing. All these activities are rituals which can help make feelings concrete. In worship, how you feel about God is made physical. It's not enough to simply *feel* certain ways about God. Worship is about *expression*. Worship is where your love feelings for God take form.

Miriam grabs a timbrel, a small hand drum with metal disks at the rim that rattle. It's very interesting that the Israelite women have their tambourines with them. The night they left Egypt was a hectic, harrowing night. Lambs were slain. The firstborn from households died. Pharaoh's army pursued. If you were trying to get out of Egypt, would your tambourine have been on your list of things to take?

The fact that Miriam and the Israelite women have their praise instruments means they have a level of faith that says, "We are going to get to the other side of this, and when we do, we need to have our instruments of worship ready."

As you go through your Red Sea, have your instruments of praise ready. Take your tambourine with you. Believe that you are going to make it through!

Miriam and the Israelite women also sing an antiphonal song, where Miriam begins and then invites them to sing the phrase she has just sung. Their expression of praise is a call and response. It is similar to how God called them out of Egypt, and how they responded by following God's call.

Singing expresses the people's praise, but they also dance. They give their bodies to the worship experience. The word for "dancing" in this passage indicates some kind of whirl and leap. It is a full-body response. It is unfortunate that many of us leave our bodies out of worship. We give our voice in singing and give our minds in contemplation, but we leave our bodies out. We give full-body responses in other parts of life. When we go to sports events, hundreds of people give full-body responses to their teams by standing up, lifting their hands, and doing the wave.

Why are we so still when we worship? What happened? It wasn't always that way. Somewhere along the line, we became more concerned about decorum than celebration.

On the day after crossing the sea, Miriam is not concerned about decorum. The Israelites recognize that God does not just bring their hearts and minds across the sea, God also brings their bodies. Whatever God has redeemed should be used in worship. God does not just save our souls; God saves our whole person. Therefore, the whole person should worship— even if it means disturbing the decorum.

When you think about what God has brought you through, let yourself play and sing and dance. The goodness of God will make you dance!

KEY POINTS

- On our journey to purpose, we should anticipate that God will accomplish great things and that His glory and grace will be recognized—not only for our own sake, but also the sake of our adversaries.

- We should realize that in shepherding our journey to purpose, God is the author and deliverer of all our blessings. Even activities that we may consider minor and insignificant are products of God's providence and can be made possible by anyone He chooses to use.

- We should remember and thank God for where He has brought us from, where we are now in the presence of His protection and provision, and when and where He will usher us into our promised destiny.

REFLECT ON THE SCRIPTURE

Then Miriam the prophet, Aaron's sister, took a timbrel in her hand, and all the women followed her, with timbrels and dancing. (Exodus 15:20)

1. What is the significance of Miriam's role and actions?

2. What is a full-body response to God?

3. How do the expressions of the Israelites' worship compare with those of our worship today?

REFLECT ON YOUR JOURNEY

1. What are the "Red Seas" in your life that God has helped you through?

2. On your journey so far, where have you experienced God's grace?

3. When do you cease to praise God—and why?

4. How can you thank God for a current blessing on your journey to purpose?

5. Who are the "Miriams" in your life who have gotten (or are getting) you where you are supposed to be? How can you thank them?

6. When have you been on *that* side of trouble? Has God brought you to *this* side (the safe and dry side) yet?

7. Where on your journey can you dance because of God's hand in your life? Can you dance today? What is it going to take for you to be able to dance?

PRAYER FOR THE JOURNEY

Gracious God, our comfort and our refuge, we come before You with grateful hearts for guiding us and encouraging us on this journey to purpose. We are eternally aware that, as a God of grace and mercy, You are the giver of every good and perfect gift. Nothing that we have received should be taken for granted. Thank you, Lord, for planting people in our lives who have been instruments of Your will. We pray that the gifts You have placed in us will be used to encourage others to glorify You. Forgive us when we fail to acknowledge Your presence and power in our lives. Fill us with a spirit of gratitude for all that You have done, all that You are doing, and all that You have promised to do. We praise, honor, and exalt You with our hearts, minds, souls, and bodies. We pray this in Christ's name and for His sake. Amen.

CHAPTER 10

A Bittersweet Journey

It would have been tempting to end the book of Exodus with the crossing of the Red Sea. Everything that follows almost seems anticlimactic. What else is there to read?

There is, in truth, much more to the story. The crossing of the Red Sea was a score, but it was not a win. The Israelites danced after crossing the Red Sea. When God enables you to come out of something that others are not able to come out of, God's goodness can make you want to sing and dance.

However, you can only dance for so long. After you score and you celebrate for a moment, it's time to get back to work. God enables you to make progress toward your destination, and the temptation is to settle for that score. You've gotten closer to your purpose, but you shouldn't settle for a score when the goal is to win.

Let's revisit the Waters of Marah and Elim. Reread Exodus 15:22-25.

THE RED SEA HAS BEEN CROSSED, BUT THE JOURNEY IS NOT OVER.

The fact that Israel makes it out of Egypt does not mean that they have "made it." God has more in store for them. Journeying "out of" is one thing; journeying "into" is something else. God is a God of complete salvation, able to deliver "out of" and "into."

According to the prophet Isaiah, God does not just take away the ashes, He gives beauty in place of the ashes.

The Spirit of the Sovereign Lord is on me, because the Lord has anointed me to proclaim good news to the poor. He has sent me to bind up the brokenhearted, to proclaim freedom for the captives and release from darkness for the prisoners, to proclaim the year of the Lord's favor and the day of vengeance of our God, to comfort all who mourn, and provide for those who grieve in Zion— to bestow on them a crown of beauty instead of ashes, the oil of joy instead of mourning, and a garment of praise instead of a spirit of despair. They will be called oaks of righteousness, a planting of the Lord for the display of his splendor. (Isaiah 61:1-3)

God brings you out of sorrow into joy, out of addiction into redemption, and out of chaos into peace. You can celebrate God for what He has brought you out of, but you can also praise God for what He has brought you into.

The Israelites score by making it out of Egypt, but now it's time to continue the journey toward their purpose. When God first commissions Moses, God does not just tell him to lead the people out of Egypt. God also promises to deliver them into a land flowing with milk and honey. However, you don't just jump into the Promised Land right after having been liberated from Egypt.

Getting from the Red Sea to the Promised Land is a pilgrimage. The people embrace the "not yet" first by following Moses out of Egypt and then by commencing a long journey toward the Promised Land.

Just because you decide to venture toward your purpose doesn't mean it will happen overnight. God will plant dreams in your spirit, but getting there is a journey filled with bitters and sweets. Exodus 3 foreshadows the journey ahead of the Israelites and us today.

'And I have promised to bring you up out of your misery in Egypt into the land of the Canaanites, Hittites, Amorites, Perizzites, Hivites and Jebusites—a land flowing with milk and honey. ...

157

But I know that the king of Egypt will not let you go unless a mighty hand compels him. So I will stretch out my hand and strike the Egyptians with all the wonders that I will perform among them. After that, he will let you go.' (Exodus 3: 17, 19-20)

When you follow Jesus and shift toward the *not yet*, you will know both bitters and sweets. We have to walk by faith and recognize that God is able to transform the one into the other.

DON'T MISS OUT ON THE PROMISED LAND BECAUSE OF THE DESOLATION OF THE DESERT.

With the memory of victory fresh in their minds, the people of God enter the desert.

Then Moses led Israel from the Red Sea and they went into the Desert of Shur. For three days they traveled in the desert without finding water. (Exodus 15:22)

After this trek into the desert, the mood is dramatically altered. Dancers and singers are stopped in their tracks. The promise falls short. This isn't the land flowing with milk and honey. Geographically, it's only 30 miles from the eastern shore of the Red Sea to the Desert of Shur, but in that short distance the Israelites go from the celebration by the sea to the desolation of the desert.

It doesn't take long to arrive in the desert after you've been by the sea. You can find yourself in the desert after one phone call, one visit to the doctor, or one pink slip.

Now, the Israelites did not just stumble upon the desert. They are led to the desert by Moses who was being led by God. Traveling into the desert is not an accident; it's a part of the journey. You can't avoid the desert. To get where you want to be, you have to deal with some deserts.

Some of your stops look nothing like where God is taking you. The temptation is to become discouraged about the desert because it doesn't support the promise. In the desert, you might be broke, confused, or alone, but keep the faith because the desert is only a stop along the way.

IF YOU TRUST GOD WITH YOUR STEPS, TRUST GOD ALSO WITH YOUR STOPS.

After crossing the Red Sea, the Israelites camp out for some time on the eastern shore. This spot is the only green spot in the northern part of the Sinai Peninsula. It is the only place where water could be obtained. Even to this day, country houses are built and gardens are laid out in that area by the richest inhabitants of the Suez.

The Israelites could have settled there and done well. On that shore, they could have had a sense of security. However, they would have missed out on the best of their purpose by simply settling for the good of their purpose.

By settling, you can avoid pain, anxiety, and uncertainty, but you also miss out on God's best.

The Israelites choose to follow God and Moses. They leave the only place where water is accessible to journey into a land where there is no water. For three days, they travel the desert and find no water. There is nothing for the people or their livestock to drink. They are thirsty now. All they can think about is water.

From a distance, they see what look like palm trees. This appears to a sign! Palm trees indicate the presence of water. The trees raise the people's level of expectation.

When they came to Marah, they could not drink its water because it was bitter. (That is why the place is called Marah.) (Exodus 15:23)

The hearts of the Israelites sink. What looks like a promising situation turns out to be just the opposite. It's even worse because it looked so promising! Expectations had been raised. They then have to deal with the disappointment of being let down.

The area they come to is a place which comes to be called Marah (the Hebrew word for "bitter"). The Israelites run to the spring and attempt to drink. What looks sweet from a distance ends up being bitter.

Some of us have been where the Israelites are in this passage. Something you think is going to bring you satisfaction ends up causing nothing but bitterness. The palm trees ahead look good, and you believe there is sweet water to be had. But you find out differently when you begin to drink.

The palm trees of that move, that job, that relationship may look promising, and then you take one drink—bitterness! Some of us have been tricked by the palm trees. Be careful of building your excitement about something or someone based on the palm trees. Drink the water first!

DISAPPOINTING WATERS CAN LEAD TO A DESTRUCTIVE BITTERNESS.

America has known times of disappointing waters, such as race riots and conflicts. The race riots of 1943 in Detroit were caused by discrimination in the automobile industry. The Watts riots of 1961 started at a Los Angeles intersection when Marquette Frye, an African American motorist was pulled over for reckless driving, then escalated into a fight with police and six days of civil unrest. Multiple riots in 1968 were spurred by the death of Martin Luther King, Jr. The Ferguson riots in 2014 began the day after the fatal shooting of Michael Brown by police officer Darren Wilson in Ferguson, Missouri. The Baltimore riots in 2015 started because of the death of Freddie Gray, a 25-year-old African American who sustained neck and spine injuries during his arrest and transport in a police vehicle.

At the core of most of these violent encounters was the reality that African Americans had come to the promising waters of justice and found nothing but the insipid taste of injustice. Bitterness is often the result of that kind of disappointment. Throughout history, the palm trees of rhetoric, political promises, and a black president looked promising. But, a drink from the waters reveals its true nature—bitterness!

FAITH HAS TO BE CONNECTED TO SOMETHING BIGGER THAN SUPPLY;
FAITH HAS TO BE CONNECTED TO THE SUPPLIER.

The Israelites attempt to drink from the water, but it's too bitter.

So the people grumbled against Moses, saying, "What are we to drink?" (Exodus 15:24)

That's not just a question; it's a statement of despair. The people are fearful because they know that if they don't find water, they and their livestock will die. They had probably taken water with them from where they had camped, but now the water has run out—and so has their faith. As in so many examples in Exodus, the Israelites' faith is connected to their supply.

God has just gotten the Israelites through something bigger than what they were going through. But how soon they forget! After just three days, they are anxious about not having water when God has just brought them through a sea of water. If God could bring them safe and dry through a sea of water, surely God could supply a drink of water.

When it comes to God, we sometimes have a "What have you done for me lately?" mentality. We forget that we've already come through something bigger than our present circumstances. The God of the Red Sea is also the God of Marah. If God can deal with a sea, He can handle a spring. God is with us in the disappointing waters of race riots and conflicts, and He will lead us to the place where we can drink the waters of justice and peace. If God has brought you through a Red Sea, don't let a small spring of bitter water make you give up on the journey.

When the Israelites cry out to Moses, Moses cries out to the Divine Supplier. The Hebrew writers sometimes characterize prayer as "crying out to the Lord." This prayer is unrehearsed, a sorrowful heart overflowing.

Then Moses cried out to the Lord...

After Moses prays, God reveals His provision. The provision may have always been there, but Moses does not see it until he prays. Prayer directs him to the answer.

...Then Moses cried out to the Lord, and the Lord showed him a piece of wood. He threw it into the water, and the water became fit to drink. (Exodus 15:25)

Sometimes our complaints can blind us, but prayer can open up our eyes. Sometimes the answer is right in front of us, but we just can't see the possibilities. Pray to God; He may open up your eyes. There are no miracles without prayer!

God shows Moses a piece of wood from a tree. There's been much speculation about what kind of wood this was and what kind of tree it had come from. Across the world several trees are known for making bitter water sweet—the hellimaram of Coromandel, the sassafras of Florida, the yerba mate of Peru, and the perru nelli of India (*A Historical and Critical Commentary on the Old Testament: Exodus* by Moritz Markus Kalisch). But none of these trees grew in that area.

The story is intentionally silent on the type of tree. As a matter of fact, it's not even a tree; it's a piece of wood—a dead piece of wood disconnected from the life of the tree. The power is not in the natural ability of the tree or the wood. The tree is only the medium that God uses. God endows the tree with the power to sweeten bitter water. If you ask, "What kind of wood is this?" you are asking the wrong question. The question is, "What kind of God is this?"

It shouldn't surprise us that God can do so much with a dead piece of wood. God later demonstrates what marvelous work He can do with two dead pieces of wood formed in the shape of a cross. That cross was thrown into the bitter waters of damnation, alienation, and sin. The power of God makes that same cross change the bitter waters of sin into the sweet waters of salvation.

The journey of life is characterized by bitters and sweets; you have to walk by faith through both flavors. God is able to transform the most bitter water into something sweet!

Are you ready to trust God with your steps, your stops, and the bittersweet along the way?

KEY POINTS

- In our lifelong journey to purpose, we can expect to have pauses and even stops in our pilgrimage toward our final destination that cause us to experience disappointment and despair.

- Throughout the phases of our journey, sometimes a positive interruption can lead to a false sense of arrival and a negative interruption can lead to a discouragement about furthering our progress. Neither situation should prevent us from realizing that God wants us to press on to the end.

- The only way to complete our journey is to put our trust totally in God; He will see us through the bitter and the sweet to shepherd us to our ultimate purpose and journey's end.

REFLECT ON THE SCRIPTURE

Then Moses cried out to the Lord, and the Lord showed him a piece of wood. He threw it into the water, and the water became fit to drink (Exodus 15:25)

1. Why is it so difficult for the Israelites to experience the lack of water after three days in the desert?

2. Does the desert represent a broken promise on the part of God?

3. What disappointing waters have led to destructive bitterness—in scripture and in history?

REFLECT ON YOUR JOURNEY

1. What are you journeying "out of" and "into"?

2. Are you currently settling for a score when the goal is to win?

3. Where have you been led to through the desert?

4. What bitters and sweets have characterized your journey so far?

5. When has prayer opened your eyes to possibilities?

6. What kind of God is walking with you on your journey?

7. How can you keep your faith connected to the supplier vs. the supply?

PRAYER FOR THE JOURNEY

Gracious and merciful God, we come humbly before You to thank You for keeping our hand in your hand, for holding onto us when we did not have the presence of mind to hold onto You. Lord, we realize that it is only Your love for us that has guided and moved us along on our journey to purpose. Your Word and Your Holy Spirit have been a lamp for our feet, leading us out of darkness into Your marvelous light. Help us to keep our hearts fixed on You and the place You want us to be. Forgive us for settling on the temporary triumphs that distract us from pursuing Your goals. Forgive us for wallowing in the depths of our disappointments when we feel that circumstances have destroyed our hope of reaching our destination. We pray that every day you will strengthen our faith and guide us on this path to purpose. With our hearts, souls, and minds, we express our gratitude to You and commit ourselves to the completion of this glorious journey. Lord, we love You and pray this in Christ's name. Amen.

CHAPTER 11

GOD WILL SUPPLY

The experience at Marah is intended to teach the Israelites that the pilgrimage from where they are to where God wants them to be includes the bitters and the sweet. Soon after crossing the Red Sea, the Israelites are led into the desert where they have to deal with the reality of an extreme scarcity of drinking water. Unimaginable thirst grips them. They see promising palm trees but discover only bitter water. In despair, they grumble against Moses and confront him with a barrage of questions. Moses turns to God who shows him a piece of wood and tells him to throw it into the water. The mighty hand of God transforms the bitter water into sweet water.

So, what comes next? Read Exodus Chapter 16.

A LEAN SEASON CAN MAKE YOU WONDER IF GOD REALLY CARES.

No matter how much the Israelites are blessed by that experience, they have to move on.

The whole Israelite community set out from Elim and came to the Desert of Sin, which is between Elim and Sinai, on the fifteenth day of the second month after they had come out of Egypt. (Exodus 16:1)

Not too long after the water shortage issue, they run into another problem. The desert environment is harsh; it offers no food possibilities—no vegetation and no grazing animals. What they brought with them has run out and what is around them offers no solution.

In the desert the whole community grumbled against Moses and Aaron. The Israelites said to them, "If only we had died by the Lord's hand in Egypt! There we sat around pots of meat and ate all the food we wanted, but you have brought us out into this desert to starve this entire assembly to death." (Exodus 16:2–3)

The Israelite pilgrims are experiencing a season of leanness.

If it isn't one thing, it's another. One bill is paid, and here comes another. One health issue is resolved, and then something else goes wrong.

It's really no surprise that the Israelites start complaining. They direct their complaints toward Moses and Aaron, but their real issue, even if they don't articulate it, is with God. God got them in this mess. He seduced them with hope for the Promised

Land. Now they find themselves in the middle of nowhere. But they can't get to God, so they lash out at the people who are within reach. Moses and Aaron become the objects of their bitterness and discontent. They are not the cause of the Israelites' problem, but they are more accessible than God is.

The fact that the Israelites complain is not surprising. What is surprising is the content of their complaint. They say they would rather stay slaves in Egypt than deal with this present crisis. Looking back to Egypt, they remember that they at least had three square meals a day. They imply that they would rather have satisfaction with oppression, than starvation with freedom. Once they are set free, staying free is hard. God sets us free, but staying free is up to us. It requires work!

The Israelites' physical bodies are on the path toward the Promised Land, but their minds are still in Egypt. At this point on their journey, security is more important than fulfilling their purpose. If living in God's will means insecurity, the Israelites would rather leave their purpose and God's promise unfulfilled in order to hold onto security. The contentment of security is hard to let go of, even when the exhilarating voice of the future is summoning you forward.

But the Israelites have selective memories. They remember the food they had in Egypt, but they forget about the harsh labor and the whole ordeal of making bricks without straw. It is tempting to romanticize the past when the present presents you with some bitters.

The Israelites want to go back because they are experiencing a season of deprivation (not having enough). A season like this can erode your faith. You may know something about lean seasons when it seems like you don't have enough to make it—not enough money, food, or work. What led you out of those seasons?

WHEN YOU DON'T HAVE ENOUGH OR WHEN WHAT IS AROUND YOU CAN'T MEET YOUR NEEDS, GOD REVEALS HIMSELF AS A SUPPLIER AND PROVIDER.

The Israelites are complaining about what they don't have, even when God has already been so good to them. He brought them out of Egypt, opened up the Red Sea, and changed bitter water into sweet. Yet, in the midst of a new crisis, the people complain once again. Their food crisis leads to a faith crisis.

Now we can't be too hard on the Israelites. How often do *we* complain—no matter how good

God has been or how recent our experience of God's provision?

But, after hearing all of the grumbling and complaining, God doesn't respond in the way that we might expect. He doesn't lose patience with or give up on the Israelites. Instead, He provides.

Then the Lord said to Moses, "I will rain down bread from heaven for you. The people are to go out each day and gather enough for that day. In this way I will test them and see whether they will follow my instructions. On the sixth day they are to prepare what they bring in, and that is to be twice as much as they gather on the other days."
(Exodus 16:4–5)

God steps in as a provider and supplier. He continues to amaze the Israelites. God could have responded by scolding and correcting them. Instead, God declares how much He is going to bless them.

At the core of our faith is the belief that God's supply is rooted in grace. The Israelites do not deserve what God is sending them. We do not deserve the blessings God sends us.

The magnitude and multiplicity of God's blessings correspond to God's gracious character. The provision says more about God than it does about us.

There is a story about a beggar by the roadside who had the nerve to ask Alexander the Great for some spare change. The beggar was poor and raggedy and had no right to ask for anything from the Emperor, yet the Emperor gave him several gold coins. One of Alexander's assistants asked, "Sir, copper coins would have adequately met the beggar's need. Why did you give him gold?" Alexander responded in royal fashion, "Copper coins would suit the beggar's need, but gold coins suit Alexander's giving."

God gives to us graciously and abundantly not because of who we are, but because of *who God is*. Big blessings suit a big God. Even when copper would do, God sends gold!

God tells Moses that He is going to rain down food from heaven. This is direct, divine intervention. God could have arranged to supply the Israelites through normal means, perhaps by showing them another piece of "wood" like He did at the waters of Marah.

Then Moses cried out to the Lord, and the Lord showed him a piece of wood. He threw it into the water, and the water became fit to drink. (Exodus 15:25)

God does not always start off with the miraculous. God's first move may be very ordinary. God can and does supply you through medicine, your job, or other people. But when that supply dries up, God can work in other ways.

Sometimes we want the miraculous to be God's first move. Are you looking for a miracle when you haven't even tapped into what God is doing in the ordinary? Are you asking for divine healing when you won't first take your medicine? Are you crying out to God to help you with your bills when you have not earnestly sought work?

God will work with you if you work with Him. When you turn to God in a time of true need and supplication (an honest request for help), God will supply. If ordinary means won't meet your needs, God can suspend the laws of nature to do so. When everything around you dries up, be on the lookout for the miraculous!

YOU CAN'T ALWAYS TELL WHAT IT IS THAT GETS YOU THROUGH A LEAN SEASON, BUT YOU CAN KNOW WHO GETS YOU THROUGH.

Through Moses, God tells the people He will rain down "bread from heaven" (Exodus 16:4). This white, grainy bread-like substance is later called "manna."

The people of Israel called the bread manna. It was white like coriander seed and tasted like wafers made with honey. (Exodus 16:31)

"Manna" sounds like the Hebrew word for "what is it"—which is fitting because no one can really describe what manna is. In fact, when the Israelites first saw the bread from heaven, they even said, "What is it?"

That evening quail came and covered the camp, and in the morning there was a layer of dew around the camp. When the dew was gone, thin flakes like frost on the ground appeared on the desert floor. When the Israelites saw it, they said to each other, "What is it?" For they did not know what it was. (Exodus 16:13–15)

The Israelites didn't know what manna was, but they did know who sent it. This is all they needed to know!

Throughout this chapter of Exodus, God continues to emphasize that the people are only to collect enough manna for that day.

"... The people are to go out each day and gather enough for that day. In this way I will test them and see whether they will follow my instructions." (Exodus 16:4)

God even specifies how much to collect, an omer, which is about 3 pounds or 1.4 kilograms.

"This is what the Lord has commanded: 'Everyone is to gather as much as they need. Take an omer for each person you have in your tent.'" (Exodus 16:16)

They are not to hoard it or store it.

Then Moses said to them, "No one is to keep any of it until morning." (Exodus 16:19)

Why is God so adamant about just getting enough for the day? Maybe it's because if the Israelites get too much, they will start depending on the manna instead of on God. They will not learn to lean on God if they already have their manna.

God is trying to nurture the Israelites' sense of dependence on God. They need to be reminded that they need God every step of the way. So, God removes all false dependence. They could not go to sleep knowing that they had food for the next morning. They would have to see what God would do the next day. The peace of their sleep becomes dependent not on what they can provide, but on what comes from heaven.

God wants us to trust God more than we trust what God provides. Our faith is not in the manna; our faith is in the God who provides the manna. Manna comes and goes; it's temporary.

However, even now, some of the Israelites disobey.

However, some of them paid no attention to Moses; they kept part of it until morning, but it was full of maggots and began to smell. (Exodus 16:20)

Perhaps God only wants them to get enough for the day to guard against greed. If they could gather more than they needed for that day, the strongest would get more and the weakest would get less. A system of Social Darwinism would develop, and eventually only the strong would survive. Hoarding leads to disparity. One of the reasons for the growing gap between rich and poor in the world is because some people, or some nations, are gathering more manna than they need and storing it away. Those in developing nations are barely subsisting because stronger nations gather up the manna faster!

The other reason that God only wants them to get enough food for the day is to simply teach them the discipline of dailiness (as in "daily-ness"— the existing state of the day). God does not want them to worry about what will happen tomorrow; God wants them to live in the provision of today. Tomorrow will take care of itself.

LIVING LIFE WITH A SENSE OF DAILINESS IS A DISCIPLINE.

Jesus said that, when we pray, we ought to pray these words:

Give us today our daily bread. (Matthew 6:11)

Jesus also says not to worry about tomorrow. The God who feeds the sparrows will feed you.

"Therefore I tell you, do not worry about your life, what you will eat or drink; or about your body, what you will wear. Is not life more than food, and the body more than clothes? Look at the birds of the air; they do not sow or reap or store away in barns, and yet your heavenly Father feeds them. Are you not much more valuable than they? (Matthew 6:25-26)

It is so tempting to rob today of its joy by focusing on tomorrow's worries. There is nothing wrong with being a planner, but at the same time, you have to know how to discipline yourself to live in today. The same God who rains down manna today is able to do it tomorrow.

God is trying to show the Israelites, and us, that life is better lived in the discipline of dailiness. Go on to bed tonight and know that God will supply. There are times when God supplies in abundance, but there are other times when God supplies in sufficiency.

GOD'S SUPPLY IS MEANT TO RESULT IN GOD'S GLORY.

The Israelites are to collect enough food for the day on Sunday through Thursday. However, on Friday, they are to collect enough for two days. Friday is the only day of the week they are to gather more than enough for one day. God tells the Israelites to collect nothing on Saturday, the seventh day.

"Bear in mind that the Lord has given you the Sabbath; that is why on the sixth day he gives you bread for two days. Everyone is to stay where they are on the seventh day; no one is to go out." *(Exodus 16:29)*

When God created the world, God rested on the seventh day and set the precedent for the Sabbath, a holy day of rest. Rest is built into the cycle of life.

Rest is sacred. For the Israelites to be productive and for the land to be productive, rest is required. Our bodies become worn out, our minds become frazzled, and our souls border on exhaustion because we don't build rest into our cycle of life. If God rested on the seventh day, what makes us think that *we* don't need to rest?

Perhaps this command is given as a foreshadowing of the Sabbath as a day of worship. God doesn't want every day to be a day of consumption. God wants the Israelites to get out of the rat race of collecting manna long enough to give God glory. The God, who has been providing all week, deserves undivided attention on this one day. God does not want to compete with manna on the Sabbath. But, once again, some of the Israelites disobey.

Nevertheless, some of the people went out on the seventh day to gather it, but they found none. (Exodus 16:27)

God provides nothing because this is one day when God wants their full attention. Some of us don't find what we're looking for when we allow manna to compete with God.

Give God your full attention. For just one day a week, let the manna go. Leave the e-mails and the work for Monday. God deserves full and consistent worship on a Sabbath day. God has earned it!

God deserves our praise because God is supplying just what we need. We can praise God for food and shelter, yes, but most of all we can thank God for providing the bread of heaven, Jesus Himself. Jesus tells His disciples that He is the "bread of life."

Jesus said to them, "Very truly I tell you, it is not Moses who has given you the bread from heaven, but it is my Father who gives you the true bread from heaven. For the bread of God is the bread that comes down from heaven and gives life to the world."

"Sir," they said, "always give us this bread."

Then Jesus declared, "I am the bread of life. Whoever comes to me will never go hungry, and whoever believes in me will never be thirsty. But as I told you, you have seen me and still you do not believe. All those the Father gives me will come to me, and whoever comes to me I will never drive away. For I have come down from heaven not to do my will but to do the will of him who sent me. And this is the will of him who sent me, that I shall lose none of all those he has given me, but raise them up at the last day. For my Father's will is that everyone who looks to the Son and believes in him shall have eternal life, and I will raise them up at the last day." (John 6:32–40)

Are you ready to give God your full attention?

KEY POINTS

- Our journey to purpose requires consistent faith. There will be times when God seems to be absent, but we should realize that He is ever present, even when we cannot sense His presence.

- In seasons of scarcity or deprivation, God often uses apparent hardships and our deficiencies to show evidence of His grace and sufficiency to supply our needs.

- God works in ways that we may not always understand to fulfill our needs in a manner that will create an awareness that what He provides us is always enough and that our focus should be on *Who* is supplying rather than *what* has been supplied.

REFLECT ON THE SCRIPTURE

Then the Lord said to Moses, "I will rain down bread from heaven for you. The people are to go out each day and gather enough for that day. In this way I will test them and see whether they will follow my instructions." (Exodus 16:4)

1. How would you respond to thirst in the desert? Would you rather go back and "stay a slave in Egypt" or deal with a present crisis of scarcity?

2. Why do you think God tests the Israelites with the dailiness of manna?

3. How is God's supply rooted in grace?

REFLECT ON YOUR JOURNEY

1. When have you experienced times when security was more important than fulfilling your purpose? Are you there now?

2. How has God revealed Himself as a supplier and provider on your journey?

3. What are you hoping God will provide for you going forward?

4. If you trust God to supply you, how can you guard against greed?

5. How do you engage in Sabbath rest? Where in your life is more needed?

6. How do you engage in Sabbath worship? Where in your life is more needed?

7. Where in your life are you not giving God your full attention? What can you do to refocus on God?

PRAYER FOR THE JOURNEY

Precious Lord, forgive us when we doubt Your ability to provide and care for us. Although we do believe, we ask You to help our unbelief. Strengthen our faith, that we may become more steadfast to and unmovable from Your purpose. We are grateful for what You have done on this sometimes-perilous journey. When we look back over our lives, we honor and adore You for bringing us through innumerable toils and snares. Help us to not be content just in the victories You have won for us and the security we have known in the past; help us to trust You to carry us forward—to places we do not know but You do. Thank You for what You have already done. May Your work be revealed daily on our journey of discovery. We pray this in Christ's name. Amen.

CHAPTER 12

HANDLING THE PRESSURE

By the time we and Moses reach Exodus 17, perhaps Moses wishes that he had never heard God's voice. If there is some way for him to go back and undo that "burning bush" episode, he just might. Moses was tending sheep on the backside of the desert. It wasn't a glamorous job, but it was secure and peaceful. The sheep never talked back to him, asked him why he led them a certain way, or threatened to stone him. But Moses was living nowhere near his purpose, so God intervened. God told him to go to Pharaoh with a message, "Let my people go," and to lead His people to a Promised Land. God saves the Israelites and Moses leads them out of Egypt and across the Red Sea. The problem is that "the land flowing with milk and honey" is not next door to the Red Sea. There is a wilderness in between. In God's discussions with Moses, God only mentions deliverance from Egypt and entry into the Promised Land. God never says anything about what is in between the promise and the fulfillment. Perhaps Moses wouldn't have embarked on his journey if he had known what was in between.

But that's the point: God can't share all the details because neither Moses nor we can handle the process of the journey up front. God is gracious enough *not* to tell us the whole story in advance. If God had shown you everything connected with where He is trying to take you, you might have kept tending sheep in the backside of the desert!

God knows that Moses could not have handled all of the information up front. God knew that Moses' faith was not, at least at that moment, commensurate with the coming struggles. By the time he arrived at the struggles, his faith would be stronger. We ought to be thankful that God does not disclose the details of our pilgrimage. Today's faith is not meant to handle tomorrow's struggles; today's faith is only for today!

Read Exodus 17:1–6.

PRESSURE COMES FROM MAKING PROGRESS.

The text does not spell it out, but it's easy to imagine that Moses may be having internal regrets about ever getting involved in Egypt and the journey to the Promised Land. He's not only trying to make it through the wilderness himself, he is also trying to lead others. With each experience of bitter water and no food, the pressure is mounting.

The whole Israelite community set out from the Desert of Sin, traveling from place to place as the Lord commanded. They camped at Rephidim, but there was no water for the people to drink.

So they quarreled with Moses and said, "Give us water to drink." Moses replied, "Why do you quarrel with me? Why do you put the Lord to the test?"

But the people were thirsty for water there, and they grumbled against Moses. They said, "Why did you bring us up out of Egypt to make us and our children and livestock die of thirst?" (Exodus 17:1–3)

Pressure is real—the pressures of performance at work and at home, of trying to make ends meet, of raising children or grandchildren, of finishing projects and meeting deadlines, of simply trying to make it through life. Sometimes these pressures mount so high that they cave in on us and we feel like there is no escape.

Moses is having to deal with pressure because he and the Israelites are making progress. They are living into their purpose. There is no pressure in staying where you are and staying who you are. Pressure is associated with trying to get where God wants you to be. When you are trying to make progress, you can expect pressure. As long as you are snorkeling, you don't need scuba gear. The moment you decide to descend into deeper depths, you need more specialized equipment. The deeper you go in your faith, your career, or your purpose, the greater the pressure you will have to deal with. If you aren't encountering any pressure, maybe you are still snorkeling.

Moses and the Israelites are camping at a place called Rephidim, but there is no water. They had already been in a place called Marah where there was bitter water, but at least at Marah there was water. They go from bitter water to no water, from bad to worse.

Rephidim is the last stop before they get to Mount Sinai, also known as Mount Horeb. Mount Sinai is where God will come down and speak to them in powerful reaffirmation and revelation. But Rephidim, the place before Mount Sinai, is the site of their greatest challenge and most intense pressure.

Sometimes your last stop before a breakthrough is the most tempting place for a breakdown. That's why you can't give up in a high-pressure time. Even if the pressure is mounting to an all-time high, don't wave the white flag of surrender at Rephidim. Your Rephidim experience could be the last stop before reaching your Sinai experience.

HOW YOU HANDLE PRESSURE DETERMINES HOW YOU COME OUT OF IT.

When the Israelites had bitter water in Marah, they complained to Moses about being in a place where there was nothing to drink. In that case, they just accused Moses of leading them to the wrong place. However, the Israelites aren't passing through Rephidim, they are camping there. Again, they go to Moses, but instead of a complaint, they come with a demand. They demand that Moses give them water.

The Israelites are implying that Moses is the source of their blessing. Maybe they think that it was Moses' special power that turned that bitter water into sweet water. But Moses had nothing to do with that miracle except do what God told him to do. The Israelites are stressing because they don't know the source of their blessing. Confusion about the source of blessing leads to stress.

When you think a financial benefactor or the company you work for is the source of your blessing, stress can be the result. This is not the source of your blessing!

The Israelites don't know that Moses is not the source of the miracle; but Moses does. Moses asks them, "Why do you quarrel with me? Why do you

191

put the Lord to the test?" (Exodus 17:2). Notice how Moses shifts the responsibility. The Israelites are looking to Moses and Moses starts talking about God. Moses understands that if there is going to be any kind of miracle, God is going to have to get involved. Moses is really saying, "You come to me with the complaint, but your issue is really with God."

REFUSE TO LIVE IN PEOPLE'S EXPECTATIONS.

Moses handles the pressure by refusing to live in the Israelites' expectations. They expect him to do and be what only God can do and be.

One of the reasons we get so stressed out is because we try to live in other people's expectations of us. Some people will try to put on you, in overt and covert ways, what only God can do and be. When you worry about the fact that you can't be what people around you think you should be, your stomach will be in knots, your blood pressure will be high, and you will be tossing and turning all night long. Stress comes when we feel as if we have to live in someone else's definition of who we are and who we ought to be. Every now and then you have to know how to say to people, "I hate to disappoint you, but I can't live in your expectation or definition of me." If you don't, stress will be the result.

The Israelites are trying to impose on Moses a role that is meant for God, and Moses refuses to fall for it. Moses is aware of his limitations, even if the Israelites aren't. He is very much in touch with the fact that he cannot do it all.

No matter what your situation, you have to be honest about you, even if no one else is. You have the inside information on the reality of your limitations. You can't let the crowd force you into their expectations. If you find that you are killing yourself trying to do it all, remember that you have limitations. You are not God.

PRESSURE CAN SQUEEZE PRAYER OUT OF YOU.

How does Moses manage the pressure? What does he do when he is close to the edge? He handles it by refusing to live in people's expectations and by venting his frustrations through prayer. When the Israelites come to him with their complaint, Moses says nothing to them. Even after Moses attempts to redirect their focus to God, they keep complaining to him: "Why did you bring us up out of Egypt to make us and our children and livestock die of thirst?" (Exodus 17:3). Moses does not address the issue with those who can't do anything about it. When the pressure is on, it helps to know where to go.

Also, this is not the time for Moses to say something directly to the Israelites. With the way he is feeling, he may say the wrong thing to them.

Pressure has a way of squeezing out of you what is in you. If cussing or crankiness are in you, pressure will squeeze it out. Sometimes we plan to pray; at other times, life squeezes prayer out of us.

PRAYER AS A PRACTICE EVENTUALLY BECOMES PRAYER AS AN INSTINCT.

When the Israelites turn on him, Moses turns to God. Prayer is a natural reaction for Moses. It's become part of his natural instinct. He practiced praying in the lonely hills of Midian as he shepherded sheep. Because he has developed this habit of prayer, he knows where to turn when he is in trouble.

You have to make prayer a habit when you are not in trouble so that you know where the path is when you are in trouble. Some of us have made it out of situations bigger than we are because we knew where the path was!

Moses tells God exactly what is on his heart. He does not sugarcoat his prayer.

Then Moses cried out to the Lord, "What am I to do with these people? They are almost ready to stone me." (Exodus 17:4)

We know Moses is mad because of how he refers to the Israelites; he says, "these people." He doesn't even claim them as "my people." This is not a nice, neat prayer. He has no time for the niceties of prayer; he only has time for the necessities of prayer. God can handle the fact that the Israelites are getting on Moses' nerves and that Moses is fearful of his life. Moses does not have to sanitize his prayers.

Prayer presents an opportunity to vent to a God who can handle what others can't handle. You have to do something with your frustrations; take them to God in prayer. God can handle the bacteria, dirt, and blood on our prayers. And it doesn't matter how we say them. Syntax, diction, and subject-verb agreement do not have to be right. Just vent. Just pray!

COOPERATING WITH GOD'S WILL LEADS TO GOD'S WILL.

Prayer can be risky because you never know how God is going to respond. Without even thinking about it, we recite the words of the model prayer that Jesus teaches us:

"'Our Father in heaven, hallowed be your name, your kingdom come, your will be done, on earth as it is in heaven. Give us today our daily bread. And forgive us our debts, as we also have forgiven our debtors. And lead us not into temptation, but deliver us from the evil one.'" (Matthew 6:9–13)

We pray "your will be done" (Matthew 6:10), "Give us today our daily bread" (Matthew 6:11), and finally "And lead us not into temptation, but deliver us from the evil one" (Matthew 6:13). Those are risky prayers! Do you really want God's will to be done? Do you really want bread just for today? Do you really want to be delivered from the evil one and temptation? If you are not ready for the answer, you might not want to make the request.

When Moses prays, he receives a strange response.

The Lord answered Moses, "Go out in front of the people. Take with you some of the elders of Israel and take in your hand the staff with which you struck the Nile, and go. I will stand there before you by the rock at Horeb. Strike the rock, and water will come out of it for the people to drink." So Moses did this in the sight of the elders of Israel. And he called the place Massah and Meribah because the Israelites quarreled and because they tested

the Lord saying, "Is the Lord among us or not?"
(Exodus 17:5-7)

God says, "Go out in front of the people" (Exodus 17:5). God tells Moses to distance himself from what is stressful. Moses may have to go back to them, but for now he needs to gain a different perspective.

Sometimes you have to get away from the source of your pressure, the source of your stress. This is not to retreat; this is to regroup. You will come back, better than when you left.

God tells Moses to "take in your hand the staff with which you struck the Nile" (Exodus 17:5). This is the staff that Moses has used in other cases when the Israelites were in trouble.

When the pressure is on, you have to know how to rely on what got you through in the past. In other words, God is saying to not only distance yourself from what is stressful, but also to depend on what is reliable. The "staff" we have is God's Word. The Word opens up seas for us.

The Lord himself goes before you and will be
with you; he will never leave you nor forsake
you. Do not be afraid; do not be discouraged."
(Deuteronomy 31:8)

God is our refuge and strength, an ever-present help in trouble. Therefore we will not fear, though the earth give way and the mountains fall into the heart of the sea, though its waters roar and foam and the mountains quake with their surging. (Psalm 46:1–3)

In times past, the Israelites made it through with the power of God's Word. You can depend on that same Word to speak into your life and your purpose.

God next commands Moses to go to "the rock at Horeb" (Exodus 17:6). In Moses' time, there were plenty of rocks at Horeb, but there must have been one that Moses was familiar with. The last time Moses was in the vicinity of Horeb, he was tending sheep in Midian. This is where he met God and first received his calling.

When the pressure is on, sometimes you just have to remember where you met God. Remember when He called you. Remember how He saved you!

God then tells Moses to "strike the rock" (Exodus 17:6). This is a bit unusual. What could logically happen by striking a rock with a stick? A rock is the most inanimate substance in nature. Nothing could come from a rock.

Following our purpose is not about logic. God commands us to do some unusual things when the pressure is on. God will ask you to do things that transcend your ability to figure them out.

The text says that Moses struck the rock. The text is silent on what God does. The narrator does not have to record what God does because we know God does what God promises. God already promised that if Moses struck the rock, water would come gushing out.

God can do it. God can bring forth refreshing waters from a lifeless rock. God can bring you refreshment in the midst of pressure-filled moments.

Are you ready to ask God for what you need?

KEY POINTS

- On our journey to purpose, we can expect to encounter difficult challenges, mostly from those who have their own expectations of us. Just as Jesus taught His disciples to anticipate persecution when they became believers, anyone on a positive path to accomplish God's purpose will face external pressures.

- The only way to manage our personal pressures on our respective journeys is to rely upon God to lead us and to refuse to give in to the negative influences of people and circumstances.

- We follow God's purpose by submitting our wills to Him. We can do this most effectively by maintaining close communication with Him through prayer—not only by calling out in situations of urgency, but by cultivating a consistent and devoted practice of prayer.

REFLECT ON THE SCRIPTURE

So they quarreled with Moses and said, "Give us water to drink." Moses replied, "Why do you quarrel with me? Why do you put the Lord to the test?" (Exodus 17:2)

1. What do the places of Massah (quarrel) and Meribah (testing) represent?

2. How are the complaints of the Israelites similar, or different, compared to the complaints of the world today?

3. What are the consequences of testing God—for the Israelites and for us?

REFLECT ON YOUR JOURNEY

1. What pressures are you currently experiencing or have experienced in your faith? Where are you dealing with pressure because you are making progress?

2. When have you been tempted to give up on your journey to purpose? Did you actually give up?

3. How can you move from living in other people's expectations of you to living in God's purpose for you?

4. Has God ever asked you to do "the unusual"?

5. When the pressure is on, how can you remember where you met God?

6. How can you develop a habit of prayer? How can you hone your practice of prayer into an instinct to pray?

7. How can you let God's Word speak into your life and your purpose?

PRAYER FOR THE JOURNEY

Dear God, we come before You with grateful hearts, knowing that You have brought us through dangers, seen and unseen. On this pilgrimage of life, we have encountered challenges in the past and are even now facing the influences of others and the changes in our circumstances that try to divert us from Your will and ultimate purpose. We pray earnestly that You would keep us in the palm of Your hand. Continue to provide us with Your protection, provision, and power to persevere along the path. We thank You in advance for answering our petitions. We pray this in the matchless and marvelous name of Jesus. Amen.

CHAPTER 13

LESSONS FROM THE BATTLEFIELD

Moses and the Israelites have had to deal with a tremendous amount of resistance and opposition on their way to the Promised Land and their purpose. You can't get from where you are to where God is taking you without having to deal with opposition. It's just a part of the deal; facing the enemy is a part of the journey.

We sometimes seem surprised when we encounter forces that are against us. When God's people are on the path of attempting to do God's will, we can expect to run into opposing forces. In Paul's letter to the Ephesians, we are reminded who and what we battle against.

For our struggle is not against flesh and blood, but against the rulers, against the authorities, against the powers of this dark world and against the spiritual forces of evil in the heavenly realms. (Ephesians 6:12)

You can't quit because you run into opposition. In fact, you may want to celebrate the opposition. That's right—celebrate! Because opposition is sometimes confirmation that you are headed in the right direction, God's direction. As a common saying goes: "If you never run into the enemy, it may be because you are headed in the same direction." If you are following the will of God, it may be confirmed by the fact that you are challenged by the enemy.

Read about the opposition the Israelites encounter in Exodus 17:8–16.

WE ARE GOING TO FACE ENEMIES SIMPLY BECAUSE WE ARE GOD'S PEOPLE.

At Rephidim, the Amalekites attack God's people. No explanation is given as to why the Amalekites do so. Maybe they still have a long-standing, deep-seated resentment against the Israelites because of the conflict between two brothers, Esau and Jacob. Jacob and Esau are the sons of Isaac (son of Abraham) and Rebekah. Genesis 27 tells the story of the stolen blessing.

Rebekah said to her son Jacob, "Look, I overheard your father say to your brother Esau, 'Bring me some game and prepare me some tasty food to eat, so that I may give you my blessing in the presence of the Lord before I die.' Now, my son, listen carefully and do what I tell you: Go out to the flock and bring me two choice young goats, so I can prepare some tasty food for your father, just the way he likes it. Then take it to your father to eat, so that he may give you his blessing before he dies." ...

Jacob said to his father, "I am Esau your firstborn. I have done as you told me. Please sit up and eat some of my game, so that you may give me your blessing." ...

After Isaac finished blessing him, and Jacob had scarcely left his father's presence, his brother Esau came in from hunting. ...

Esau held a grudge against Jacob because of the blessing his father had given him. ...
(Genesis 27:6-10, 19, 30, 41)

The Amalekites are the descendants of the great grandson of Esau and the Israelites are the descendants of Jacob. At this point, the Amalekites may not even know why they are feuding with the Israelites. They just believe they should be because their ancestors did.

Much violence in our world is nonsensical because it is based on inherited issues that have nothing to do with contemporary times. There are some Israelis who probably don't even know why they don't like Arabs or white people who may not even know why they have issues with black people, and vice versa. There are some people with whom you have conflict, and the reason for the conflict is not even known!

Perhaps the Amalekites see the gradual prosperity of the Israelite people and are envious of it. The Israelites, even through all of their struggles, are being blessed simply because they are God's people. As God's people, we will have enemies because of our identity.

EVERY BATTLE THAT GOD EXPOSES US TO IS MEANT TO INSTRUCT US.

We don't know why the Amalekites attack, but they do.

The Amalekites came and attacked the Israelites at Rephidim. Moses said to Joshua, "Choose some of our men and go out to fight the Amalekites. Tomorrow I will stand on top of the hill with the staff of God in my hands."

So Joshua fought the Amalekites as Moses had ordered, and Moses, Aaron and Hur went to the top of the hill. As long as Moses held up his hands, the Israelites were winning, but whenever he lowered his hands, the Amalekites were winning. When Moses' hands grew tired, they took a stone and put it under him and he sat on it. Aaron and

Hur held his hands up—one on one side, one on the other—so that his hands remained steady till sunset. So Joshua overcame the Amalekite army with the sword. (Exodus 17:8-13)

Moses commands Joshua to choose an army. Joshua is not to ask for volunteers; he is to choose the soldiers. They battle the Amalekites while Moses stands on the mountain holding the staff of God.

When Moses gets tired, he is helped by a different kind of staff—his support staff, Hur and Aaron. They literally lift up Moses' hands. The role of Moses' leadership team is to lift him up when he is weary. In this battle, one person fights the enemy with his "hands up," supported by other people who fight with their "hands under," while most of the Israelites fight with their "hands on." Because everyone works together in their roles, they are victorious over the Amalekites.

REVELATION OCCURS IN THE BATTLE.

Exodus 17 then describes what Moses and the Israelites learn from their battle.

Then the Lord said to Moses, "Write this on a scroll as something to be remembered and make sure that Joshua hears it, because I will completely blot out the name of Amalek from under heaven."

Moses built an altar and called it The Lord is my Banner. He said, "Because hands were lifted up against the throne of the Lord, the Lord will be at war against the Amalekites from generation to generation." (Exodus 17:14–16)

Every battle in our lives should teach us something. Struggles are not to be wasted. We ought to come away with knowledge once a battle is over. There are some things that formal education from an institution of higher learning can't teach you. For example, you might earn a degree that does not come from a classroom, such as a bachelor's degree from the institute of tribulation, a master's degree from the school of hard knocks, or a PhD from the university of adversity.

The struggles the Israelites go through in the wilderness are meant to teach them. God exposes them to struggle so that God can shape them for what is next.

The last thing you want to do is go through a storm and come out of it with nothing learned. After military conflicts, armed forces leaders will meet to debrief the previous battles and discuss what they have learned. After a struggle, you may want to debrief yourself and document what you have learned.

GOD IS AT WORK BEHIND THE SCENES.

After the battle, the first thing out of Moses' mouth is "The Lord is...." Now he could have come out of the battle saying, "I am...," because he is the one who has to hold up the staff. Moses does a good job at standing where he can be seen to be a source of inspiration for those fighting in the trenches. Moses could have come out of the battle saying, "Joshua is...," because Joshua is worthy of a medal of honor for mustering and mobilizing the troops for war. Joshua also courageously engages in hand-to-hand combat. Moses could also have come out of the battle saying, "Aaron and Hur are...," because without them Moses wouldn't have had the physical support he needed to accomplish his job.

Moses knows that nothing would have happened if God was not working behind the scenes. Moses was "hands up"; Aaron and Hur were "hands under"; Joshua was hands on; but God was hands over! Competence plus divine intervention is what leads to victory.

No matter how good you are at whatever you do, if God is not working behind the scenes, nothing is going to happen. Sometimes God is working behind your work, and you don't even know it. You might think that the battles you've won have been because of your fighting alone. The truth is that

God has been making calls behind the scenes to work in your favor.

GOD IS OUR BANNER IN OUR BATTLES.

Moses comes out of this battle declaring, "The Lord is my Banner." God is "Jehovah Nissi," or "Jehovah my banner." This expression becomes a proper name for God in the Old Testament.

In historical battles, opposing nations would fly their flag on a pole at their respective front lines. The purpose of this flag was to give soldiers a feeling of hope and a focal point.

Moses is saying, "God is my banner." God is the banner flown in a visible place to provide hope and encouragement for those on the battlefield. When you are in the midst of the fight, it helps to be able to look up and see the source of your hope.

I lift up my eyes to the mountains— where does my help come from? My help comes from the Lord, the Maker of heaven and earth. (Psalm 121)

Moses comes out of the battle with this declaration about God: God is my banner. He doesn't discover this from his home life or school. It takes the battlefield to give him this revelation.

In scripture, most revelation about God occurs in crises. It's only after the bitter water is turned sweet in Exodus 15 that the Israelites discover that God is "Jehovah Rapha," the God who heals. It's only after the battle with the Amalekites in Exodus 17 that the Israelites discover that God is "Jehovah Nissi," the God who is my banner.

It's the same for us. Most of the revelations about God will come amidst the battles we face on our journey to purpose. The opposition that we encounter is the opportunity for God to reveal Himself to us. When you are deep in the fight, look to the banner of God.

PRAYER IS NECESSARY ON THE BATTLEFIELD.

When Joshua and the soldiers are fighting on the battlefield, Moses positions himself on top of a hill. He holds his staff in his hands and lifts his hands toward heaven. Lifting hands toward heaven is symbolic of a dependence on God. Lifting hands is also a sign of intercession. With hands held high, Moses intercedes on behalf of those who are engaged in battle. When Moses' hands are lifted high, the Israelite soldiers are winning the battle. When he gets tired and his hands drop, they start losing. Winning or losing the battle below is influenced by what Moses is doing above. The fight occurs in both venues—on the battlefield where Joshua and the Israelite soldiers fight and on the hill where Moses prays.

The fighting in the field and praying on the hill go together. There is no praying alone and there is no fighting alone. Praying without fighting is fantasy; fighting without praying is futile.

Before Jesus fights the enemy on the cross, he first makes his way to the Garden of Gethsemane.

Then Jesus went with his disciples to a place called Gethsemane, and he said to them, "Sit here while I go over there and pray." He took Peter and the two sons of Zebedee along with him, and he began to be sorrowful and troubled. Then he said to them, "My soul is overwhelmed with sorrow to the point of death. Stay here and keep watch with me."

Going a little farther, he fell with his face to the ground and prayed, "My Father, if it is possible, may this cup be taken from me. Yet not as I will, but as you will." (Matthew 36–39)

There are times when you have to fight as though it's all up to you while simultaneously praying as though it's all up to God. To only fight may indicate a lack of faith in God. To only pray may indicate a lack of acting in faith for God's purpose for you.

In the Civil Rights movement, marchers and protesters did not rush right to the streets; they first went to mass meetings in the church where they prayed. One of the reasons that the current fight for justice has not been as effective is because younger generations want to rush to the streets to declare "black lives matter" without first going to the church to talk to God.

As a matter of fact, praying is a form of fighting. The activity on the hill of prayer is as much a war room as the battlefield. A war room is a place from which a war is directed; it can also be a place where business or political strategy is planned. The movie "War Room" is a 2015 Christian drama directed by Alex Kendrick who said, "We called it 'War Room' because, like the military, we should seek God for the right strategy before going into combat. By combat, I mean daily issues we face in our culture."

Battles at work, at home, and in your own spirit are won in the war room. The reason we have to keep fighting certain battles without any sense of progress is because we get mixed up about where the war room is. The war room is not just the board room at work; it might be the bathroom where you pray before you go to the board room.

Prayer is a way of doing battle. Some of us have a Joshua spirit to fight instead of a Moses spirit to pray. For optimal results, the Joshua spirit and the Moses spirit have to work together. Prayer doesn't always take the place of what Joshua has to do, but it does make Joshua's job easier!

WORSHIP AT THE ALTAR WILL PREPARE YOU FOR THE NEXT BATTLE.

After the fighting is done and the battle is won, Moses builds an altar. Altars can be a place of sacrifice, of worship, or both. In Exodus 17:15, Moses builds an altar as a place of thanksgiving and worship. The place of war now becomes the place of worship.

It would have been very tempting for Moses and the Israelites to simply go off and enjoy the spoils of victory after having won the battle. After a major victory, you are supposed to indulge in the win. Moses, however, opts to worship.

When God gives you a victory, it's time to build an altar. Warriors need to become worshipers. You've been on the battlefield all week. At the very least, praise and worship God on a Sunday, on a Sabbath, on the day after the battle.

After Moses names the altar, he then acknowledges that the war is not over:

Moses built an altar and called it The Lord is my Banner. He said, "Because hands were lifted up against the throne of the Lord, the Lord will be at war against the Amalekites from generation to generation." (Exodus 17:15-16)

God will be at war; God's people will still be at war. There are more hills to climb and more battles to fight. The Amalekites are still around, but God is worthy of praise because of what He brings us through.

Your journey is not over. Your purpose is not yet fulfilled. But God is worthy because His hands are over you. Jesus tells his disciples and us:

"I have told you these things, so that in me you may have peace. In this world you will have trouble. But take heart! I have overcome the world." (John 16:33)

You don't have to wait until the battle is over, you can shout now, "God is worthy!"

Are you ready to overcome?

KEY POINTS

- Our journey to purpose may be hindered by perceived obstacles, but these very obstacles can be vehicles that enable and enhance our spiritual growth.

- As we face and overcome challenges, God reveals Himself as the force behind our victories and the faithful responder to our prayers.

- Progress on our journey is impossible without prayer. Prayer not only provides us with the opportunity to praise and worship God for His present help, but to prepare us for future battles.

REFLECT ON THE SCRIPTURE

Moses built an altar and called it The Lord is my Banner. (Exodus 17:15)

1. What are the spiritual forces in opposition to God's will?

2. How is prayer a form of fighting?

3. How do the enemies and opposition that the Israelites face shape their relationship with God?

4. What is the significance of a revelation in the midst of a battle?

REFLECT ON YOUR JOURNEY

1. When have you been challenged by the enemy? What was the outcome?

2. Who or what supports you on the battlefield?

3. Where has God been at work behind the scenes for you?

4. What is your "war room" or place of prayer? How can you make prayer a more permanent part of your journey?

5. When do you go to the "altar of worship" to praise and thank God? Are there places along your journey where you might need to stop to praise and thank God?

6. What has God exposed you to that might be shaping you for what is next?

PRAYER FOR THE JOURNEY

Lord, You have been our dwelling place in all generations. As we advance along our journey to purpose, we become increasingly aware that it is Your abiding presence that enables us to meet the challenges that confront us. Your mighty power allows us to muster the strength to fight our continuing battles. It is only by Your mercy and Your grace that we move forward and make progress. It is Your protection that preserves us. Thank You for hearing our prayers. Thank You for Your promises to carry us to the completion of our journey. We pray this in Christ's name and for His sake. Amen.

CHAPTER 14

LITTLE BY LITTLE

Moses and the Israelites have journeyed far, in both body and spirit. They've come a long way from the "burning bush" call of God (Exodus 3), the exodus from Egypt (Exodus 12), the crossing of the Red Sea (Exodus 14), and God's provision of sweet water (Exodus 15), manna (Exodus 16), and water again, this time from a rock (Exodus 17). Through Moses, God warns the Israelites that the Promised Land of "milk and honey" (Exodus 13) is currently inhabited by their enemies, but God also promises to overcome these enemies and defeats the Amalekites at Rephidim (Exodus 17).

Even with the power and presence of God, the journey has not been easy. Read about where Moses and the Israelites are now in Exodus 23:20-32.

THE REALITY OF ADVERSITY IS PART OF THE JOURNEY.

When God tells Moses that He will bring the Israelites into a good and spacious land, a land flowing with milk and honey, God also refers to this land as the home of the Canaanites, Hittites, Amorites, Perizzites, Hivites, and Jebusites. The land God has promised them is occupied by other people and not just any other people; it's occupied by their enemies.

God does not hide this fact from them. Following God is not all about "milk and honey," that is, blessing, breakthrough, success, and prosperity. What the Israelites embark on *includes* milk and honey, but it's not *all about* milk and honey.

Going where God leads you includes dealing with enemies and going through suffering and sacrifice. Jesus never hides this fact.

Then he said to them all: "Whoever wants to be my disciple must deny themselves and take up their cross daily and follow me. (Luke 9:23)

"I have told you these things, so that in me you may have peace. In this world you will have trouble. But take heart! I have overcome the world." (John 16:33)

Some people give up on their path to purpose because in their pursuit of the milk and honey of the faith, they run into hardships, seasons of suffering, and enemies. Don't give up! It's part of the journey. God is with you every step of the way. He can even send you an angel to prepare the way.

"See, I am sending an angel ahead of you to guard you along the way and to bring you to the place I have prepared. Pay attention to him and listen to what he says. Do not rebel against him; he will not forgive your rebellion, since my Name is in him. If you listen carefully to what he says and do all that I say, I will be an enemy to your enemies and will oppose those who oppose you. My angel will go ahead of you and bring you into the land of the Amorites, Hittites, Perizzites, Canaanites, Hivites and Jebusites, and I will wipe them out. Do not bow down before their gods or worship them or follow their practices. You must demolish them and break their sacred stones to pieces. Worship the Lord your God, and his blessing will be on your food and water. I will take away sickness from among you, and none will miscarry or be barren in your land. I will give you a full life span. (Exodus 23:20-26)

LEAVE THE "HOW" UP TO GOD.

God informs Moses and the Israelites of the existence of the enemy, but God never tells them *how* the occupants of the Promised Land are going to be dealt with. Moses and the Israelites don't know how the anticipated obstacles will be handled, but they begin their pursuit of their purpose even in the face of this knowledge.

The call of God does not always come with details, specifics, and contingency plans. God does not spell out the details of how the enemy will be dealt with. God is more into disclosing the "what" than the "how." Most often, we want to know *how* it's going to happen, but we're not wise enough or strong enough to deal with *how*.

The only thing God asks us to do is get on the road. Sometimes we are blessed enough to know the *what*, but we should always leave the *how* to God.

FAITH DOES NOT MEAN LIVING IN DENIAL OF ANTICIPATED OBSTACLES; FAITH SAYS, "I'M MOVING ANYWAY."

If God promises you a place of arrival, you have to trust that God will see you through the turbulence you are likely to encounter. You may not be able to see how God is going to do it and you may not be able to figure it out based on what God tells you upfront. This is when you have to "faith it out."

To "faith it out" means you have to travel, even with the opposition in your awareness. Obstacles and enemies may be in your head, but you can't let them stop you. And just because the enemy may be in your head, doesn't mean that the enemy is in your heart. When the obstacle is only in your head, you can keep on walking. If you let the enemy into your heart, all forward progress stops. In these situations, turn to God—"faith it out"—and continue your journey.

For six and a half chapters (Exodus 17 through the first half of Exodus 23) the Israelites receive guidance on how to live, including the Ten Commandments (Exodus 20). But now, toward the end of God's conversation with Moses about the Israelites, God brings the enemies back up and describes how the obstacles will be dealt with.

"I will send my terror ahead of you and throw into confusion every nation you encounter. I will make all your enemies turn their backs and run. I will send the hornet ahead of you to drive the Hivites, Canaanites and Hittites out of your way. But I will not drive them out in a single year, because the land would become desolate and the wild animals too numerous for you. Little by little I will drive them out before you, until you have increased enough to take possession of the land. (Exodus 23:27–30)

In this part of the promise, God gives them the plan: "Little by little I will drive them out..." (Exodus 23:30). God explains that He is going ahead of the Israelites to deal with the enemy.

In turn, God tells us, "While you are journeying, I am ahead of you working."

THE JOURNEYING IS UP TO THE PEOPLE AND US; THE WORKING (THE HOW) IS UP TO GOD.

God says that He will cause the enemy to become afraid of God, not the Israelites. The fear is not a fear of other people or what these people can do; the fear is a fear of God. The occupants of the land would hear what God was doing in other places and that would cause an even greater fear of God.

It's not you that causes fear in your enemy, it's the power of God.

God deals with the enemy by invoking fear, instigating confusion, and by inciting the hornets. God uses nature against the occupants of the land. God can use whatever God chooses to use to further God's purpose. The sting of the hornet can chase some of our enemies away!

WHAT IS URGENT FOR US IS NOT AN EMERGENCY FOR GOD.

God tells the Israelites that He is going to drive out their enemies "little by little." God promises a gradual reduction of the current occupants of the land. The need of the Israelites is not going to force God into altering His timeline or rushing His plan. What may feel like an emergency to the Israelites is not necessarily an emergency to God. God views emergencies differently.

This is how God works sometimes. God does not always work all at once. God is able to do it all at once—to open up the sea and defeat the enemy all at once. But many times, God does what God does little by little. Gradually, God deals with what and who is trying to stop you or hinder your progress.

There are times when God heals little by little. We may want healing now, but God does not always work that way. In one case, Jesus heals a blind man named Bartimaeus immediately.

"What do you want me to do for you?" Jesus asked him.

The blind man said, "Rabbi, I want to see."

"Go," said Jesus, "your faith has healed you." Immediately he received his sight and followed Jesus along the road. (Mark 10:51-52)

In another case, Jesus touches a blind man twice in order to heal him.

They came to Bethsaida, and some people brought a blind man and begged Jesus to touch him. He took the blind man by the hand and led him outside the village. When he had spit on the man's eyes and put his hands on him, Jesus asked, "Do you see anything?"

He looked up and said, "I see people; they look like trees walking around."

Once more Jesus put his hands on the man's eyes. Then his eyes were opened, his sight was restored, and he saw everything clearly. (Mark 8:22–25)

In yet another case, Jesus tells a blind man that he must take action by washing himself in a pool to see again.

As he went along, he saw a man blind from birth. His disciples asked him, "Rabbi, who sinned, this man or his parents, that he was born blind?"

"Neither this man nor his parents sinned," said Jesus, "but this happened so that the works of God might be displayed in him. As long as it is day, we must do the works of him who sent me. Night is coming, when no one can work. While I am in the world, I am the light of the world."

After saying this, he spit on the ground, made some mud with the saliva, and put it on the man's eyes. "Go," he told him, "wash in the Pool of Siloam" (this word means "Sent"). So the man went and washed, and came home seeing. (John 9:1–7)

God chips away at possibility in God's way. It's not always all at once. God opens doors little by little. He empowers you to overcome temptation and accomplish your dreams little by little.

We have to learn how to rejoice in today's "little." We have to know how to survive on and appreciate today's *little*. Then we need to praise God for tomorrow's *little*. Sometimes you have to shout about the little!

SOMETIMES GOD KEEPS ONE ENEMY IN PLACE TO KEEP AWAY ANOTHER.

Why does God work little by little? Why doesn't God drive the enemy out overnight? Why doesn't God work faster and harder in *our* situation? We've heard God do it for other people.

In Exodus 23, God is working little by little to avoid the desolation of the land.

But I will not drive them out in a single year, because the land would become desolate and the wild animals too numerous for you. (Exodus 23:29)

If God drove out the enemy too much ahead of time, the land would not be the land of milk and honey that it is today. God leaves the enemies in place because their work will end up yielding a harvest for the Israelites. Sometimes the enemy does not even know that they are serving God's plan by "working some land" for you.

God left Judas, Jesus' betrayer, in the group of disciples because his work would serve God's plan. Jesus would never have died on the cross and been resurrected for us if Judas had not played his part.

If God drove out the enemy too soon, there would also be no one to keep the wild animals from taking over. The wild animals would become even worse than the present occupants. God keeps one enemy in place to keep a worse enemy from taking over.

GROW AS YOU GO!

God is also working little by little to allow for the people to "increase," both in their numbers and their faith.

Little by little I will drive them out before you, until you have increased enough to take possession of the land. (Exodus 23:30)

The Israelites have grown as they journeyed, just as we develop as we traverse the road on which God wants us to be. You don't have to wait to get to where you want to be before you grow. You can be productive on the way.

To build their strength in numbers, which would subsequently intimidate the enemy, God needed to give the Israelites some time. They weren't ready for milk and honey yet. They needed to grow before they would reach the Promised Land. They needed maturation before God's blessing.

God needs to know that our level of maturity matches the blessing in store for us. God knows what you can handle and when you can handle it. You may want God to give the blessing to you now, but you may not be ready for it.

Much later in the Old Testament, a man named Jabez prays a prayer of wisdom and blessing.

Jabez cried out to the God of Israel, "Oh, that you would bless me and enlarge my territory! Let your hand be with me, and keep me from harm so that I will be free from pain." And God granted his request. (1 Chronicles 4:10)

Before Jabez asks God to "enlarge my territory," he asks God to "bless me." In other words, "mature me before you give me Your blessings." We have to trust God's wisdom and timing. God knows how to match blessing and maturity.

TRUST THAT GOD IS WORKING IN YOUR LIFE LITTLE BY LITTLE.

God isn't sitting on the sidelines. God is still working—even if it is little by little and even it if goes undetected at times.

God is true to God's promise. For the Israelites, God details the boundaries of their blessing.

"I will establish your borders from the Red Sea to the Mediterranean Sea, and from the desert to the Euphrates River. I will give into your hands the people who live in the land, and you will drive them out before you. Do not make a covenant with them or with their gods. Do not let them live in your land or they will cause you to sin against me, because the worship of their gods will certainly be a snare to you." (Exodus 31–32)

The promise of the Promised Land still stands. The promise has to come through Red Seas, deserts, bitter waters, scarcity, and enemies—but it still stands.

Are you ready to live in God's promise for you? This is the question of the chapter. This is the question of the book. Readiness to live in God's promise is demonstrated by a willingness to journey toward purpose. The journey to purpose is not simply about fulfilling personal dreams or personal happiness. Purpose is about living in God's will and working to fulfill our God-given purpose. As this chapter declares, discovery and pilgrimage happen little by little. They do not happen suddenly. Immediate gratification is not at the center of this journey. The journey is a walk of faith in which God goes ahead of us, walks beside us, and protects us from behind.

YOUR JOURNEY TO PURPOSE CONTINUES LITTLE BY LITTLE.

This book is intended as a guide for the call, journey, and purpose that God is working in your life. As your journey continues, it may be helpful to refer back to certain chapters when the themes and scriptures reflect where you and/or your community of faith are, on the road to purpose. Just remember that God is working things out ahead of you, Jesus is walking right alongside you, and the Holy Spirit dwells within you to guide you.

KEY POINTS

- Obstacles and difficulties on our journey to purpose are necessary ingredients for the final feast of our spiritual maturation. These diversions never diminish the rewards that God has in store for us at the end of the road.

- Navigating our journey requires us to keep our focus on our final destination. We need to trust that God will manage the details and logistics of how we get there. God can use impediments, delays, and even enemies to ultimately work in our favor and enhance our individual and collective faith and growth.

- Advancement along the journey to purpose usually occurs in increments. We need to remember to not just focus on the miraculous and instantaneous blessings bestowed, but also to focus on the God who is providing the blessings to us—little by little.

REFLECT ON THE SCRIPTURE

Little by little I will drive them out before you, until you have increased enough to take possession of the land. (Exodus 23:30)

1. Why are the emergencies of the Israelites not necessarily the situations that God addresses?

2. What is the maturity level of the Israelites' faith at the end of Exodus Chapter 23 compared to what it was in the previous chapters of Exodus?

3. If God was able to provide freedom, supply, and blessings for the Israelites in the past, why doesn't God do that for us today?

4. If God is able to work miracles of healing, freedom, and salvation, why doesn't God do so when we need healing, freeing, and saving?

REFLECT ON YOUR JOURNEY

1. Right here, right now: Are you following God's purpose or plan for you? Why or why not?

2. How has your journey of faith progressed from when you first started reading this book to now?

3. Where have you encountered God along the way?

4. What can you do to increase your trust in God during times of struggle or scarcity?

5. In what areas might you need to spiritually mature?

6. While you are journeying, where could God be at work ahead of you?

PRAYER FOR THE JOURNEY

Most gracious and loving Father, we pause on this phase of our journey to purpose to say, "Thank You!" As we reflect on where You have brought us from, we are eternally grateful for Your protection and provision. We confess that we sometimes harbor doubts about Your presence and power in the middle of our darkest trials. But when we reflect on Your track record, we know we can have complete confidence in the fact that You can do all things. You turn our despair into delight. You turn our failures into fruitfulness. You even protect and bless us in the presence of our enemies. You are truly an awesome God! We pray that we will grow closer to You as You reveal to us, little by little, Your providence and Your promises on this glorious journey. Our victories, day by day, give us continuing confidence in Your divine grace and power, and our mistakes and detours give You opportunities to display Your boundless love through Your signs of grace and mercy as You guide us. To You be glory, honor, and majesty as we shout, "Hallelujah!" In Christ's name we pray. Amen!

ABOUT THE AUTHOR

REV. JERRY M. CARTER, JR., PH.D.

Dr. Jerry M. Carter, Jr. is the 14th pastor of the Calvary Baptist Church of Morristown, NJ. A faithful theologian whose commitment to articulate the gospel in both written and oratory forms has transformed and shaped the lives of generations. He is a highly sought-after revivalist, keynote speaker, lecturer, mentor and teacher who has been invited to share the gospel on numerous platforms throughout the country. He received a Bachelor of Arts degree from Denison University, in Granville, Ohio, a Master of Divinity degree from Princeton Theological Seminary, and a Doctorate of Philosophy degree from Drew University in Madison, New Jersey. He is president of the African-American Clergy Association of Morris County and the 2017 recipient of the NAACP New Jersey State Conference, Religious Leader of Excellence Award. Dr. Carter is also the founder and host of the How Shall They Hear Preaching conference and distinguished visiting professor of the Transformational Preaching Doctor of Ministry program at New Brunswick Theological

Seminary in New Brunswick, NJ. He is an author who has inspired through his published works in the New Interpreters Handbook of Preaching, Oxford Sermons Volume III, Evangelizing the Black Male in the 21st Century and the African American Pulpit. In 2015, Dr. Carter published his first book "The Empowered Life: Living Well in the Spirit" available on Amazon.com and other retail stores and outlets. Dr. Carter is a native of Columbus, Ohio, and the proud father of three children, Jerry M. III, Zachary Daniel, and Camille.

Follow Dr. Carter on Facebook, Twitter and Instagram or join his mailing list at **www.jmcarterjr.org** for news and information on upcoming events. Use the Speaker Request form on the website to invite Dr. Carter for book readings and signings, preaching workshops & seminars, revivals, conferences and conventions.

JERRY M. CARTER, JR.
MINISTRIES

Made in the USA
Middletown, DE
27 November 2019